ROYAL COMMISSION ON
HISTORICAL MANUSCRIPTS

The Prime Ministers' Papers Series

# W. E. GLADSTONE

IV: Autobiographical Memoranda 1868—1894

EDITED BY JOHN BROOKE
AND MARY SORENSEN

LONDON
HER MAJESTY'S STATIONERY OFFICE

# PREFACE

The documents printed in this fourth and concluding volume of a complete edition of Gladstone's autobiographical writings have been selected and edited for publication by Mr. John Brooke from transcripts by Mrs. M. O. Sorensen. The appended history of the Gladstone archive is the work of Dr. R. J. Olney, who has also been responsible for seeing the volume through the press.

The Commission would again wish to express its thanks to Sir William Erskine Gladstone, Bt., for his permission to publish these writings of his great-grandfather. The documents in the Royal Archives at Windsor Castle are published by gracious permission of Her Majesty the Queen.

G. R. C. DAVIS
Secretary

# CONTENTS

# CONTENTS

# INTRODUCTORY NOTE

This volume contains Gladstone's autobiographical memoranda from his first assumption of the office of Prime Minister in December 1868 to his final resignation in March 1894. From the point of view of the historian, these are the most important years of Gladstone's life; but they are not the years about which he wrote most. He was too occupied with his duties as Prime Minister and leader of the Liberal party to find time to write accounts of political conversations, unless they were needed for a record. It might be useful to set down the opinions of Chamberlain in 1887 (304) or Parnell in 1889 (307) in view of continuing negotiations with these statesmen. But Gladstone no longer felt the need to examine his own doubts on paper as he had done in the 1830s and 1840s. The only occasion on which he did so in these later years was on a family matter and an affair of conscience (284), namely the rites according to which his sister, Helen, should be buried.

The most important political memoranda date from the period of the first ministry. There is a long memorandum, together with supporting documents, on the crisis of July 1869 when the House of Commons rejected the Lords' amendments to the Irish Church Bill (277); and two of conversations with the Queen in 1871, which show the difficulties Gladstone had to face with her (278–279). A few brief memoranda on political conversations suffice for the ministry of 1880, but there is a lengthy record of the negotiations leading to the assumption of office by the Conservatives in 1885 (300). Though the memoranda are infrequent after 1885, Gladstone never entirely lost his taste for chronicling the events in which he was concerned.

His writings concerning his resignation (313–319) conclude the long story of his relations with Queen Victoria. All that Gladstone knew at the end was that the Queen disliked him; he did not know why, and if he had any suspicions he never put them down on paper. He compared himself to the mule on which he had made the tour of Sicily in 1838, and which despite its service he had grown to hate. So, too, had it been with the Queen.

The memoranda in the present volume are edited, as in previous volumes, from the Gladstone Papers in the British Library. The originals are to be found mostly in the Miscellanea series of the main collection ADD MSS 44722–44776 (see Vol. I, p. 9) but a few are amongst the supplementary papers presented in 1970. In appropriate cases related correspondence and papers concerning Cabinet meetings have been printed from elsewhere in the Gladstone Papers; and this additional material also includes unpublished papers of Queen Victoria from the Royal Archives, Windsor Castle. For help in this latter connection especial thanks are due to Miss V. J. Langton, Registrar of the Royal Archives.

JOHN BROOKE

**271**  28 November 1868  *Conversation with Lord Halifax: WEG invited to form a Ministry*
ADD MS 44756 ff 59–60

In pursuance of a letter he had addressed to me on the 25th,[1] Lord Halifax came here last evening. His object was to convey what had been made known to him through General Grey from Her Majesty.

That Lord Stanley and Mr. Disraeli desired immediate retirement if agreeable to the entire Cabinet.

That this was to be decided on Tuesday.

That Her Majesty wished me to be in possession of her objections to two persons in particular so that I might not commit myself to any one before seeing her.

Namely C[larendon] for the Foreign Office and De T[abley] for the Household office of Lord in Waiting. Two of her very old servants.

The objections were not stated but I gathered that they consisted in some disrespectful language stated to have been uttered by each respectively. The intimation was that they were very strong and the feeling which prompted them much stronger still.

Halifax said that thus appealed to he had no option but to convey them but he carefully abstained from giving any opinion upon them.

I mentioned in the case of Clarendon the singular concurrence of titles to the Foreign Office—in the case of De Tabley his being a man very careful in speech about all persons and as I find rather reticent.

I said that nothing should be done by me in this interval to create embarrassment: that I did not feel certain whether to seek some counsel before seeing Her Majesty. He was doubtful. But generally refrained from expression of opinion.

Her Majesty would like Granville at Foreign Office—Duchess of Argyll Mistress of the Robes in the event of Duchess of Wellington's resignation. If this could not be then Lady Aylesbury.

Lords not much relished, D[artre]y, C[amoy]s, C[aithne]ss. Better liked T[albot] de M[alahide], Methuen, Torr[ingto]n, (Suffield?).

---

[1] ADD MS 44814, ff 220–225. '25th' was added afterwards in pencil.

D[uke] of S[utherland] not well liked. Nor R[oxburghe]. Aylesbury might exchange with Bessborough. Sydney as before.

But all this was secondary.

The main subject perplexed me much.

*Hawarden. November 29. 1868.*

**272** 2 December 1868 *Projected memorandum for the Queen: assurances to be given by Lord Clarendon*
ADD MS 44756 ff 63–64

*Secret.*

Mr. Gladstone about six months ago mentioned to Lord Clarendon his hope that in the event of a change of government Lord Clarendon would consent to be named to Her Majesty for the Foreign Office.

Mr. Gladstone at once states his belief that his formation of a government need not absolutely depend upon the fulfilment of this hope.

But he feels that the public expectation will fix itself on Lord Clarendon as Foreign Minister and that if any other arrangement be made it will be ascribed directly to the Sovereign.

In his opinion *this* would be a serious evil.

He asks himself whether it might not be possible that Lord Clarendon might, without entering upon any controversy or argument whatever, submit to Her Majesty declarations and assurances which might be satisfactory and which no gentleman would more loyally, or more carefully, fulfil, so as to set Her Majesty entirely at her ease, and to establish those relations with the Foreign Secretary which are absolutely necessary.

Were it Her Majesty's pleasure to permit this course to be pursued, inconveniences would be avoided which it is Mr. Gladstone's duty to point out as probable in any other contingency.

*Hawarden. December 2. 1868.*

*Docketed by secretary:* Projected. December 2/68.

**273** 2 December 1868 *Conversation with General Grey: the position of Lord Clarendon*
ADD MS 44756 ff 61–62

General Grey arrived from Windsor today with Her Majesty's letter.[1]

---

[1] Philip Guedalla, ed., *The Queen and Mr. Gladstone*, 1933, i. no. 75.

I pointed out to him the matters detailed in the short memorandum herewith.[1] He *felt* the difficulty, that the supercession will be ascribed to Her Majesty. He telegraphed in cipher to Her Majesty and requested an audience for me at Windsor tomorrow.

I pointed out that prior consultations would not be expedient, as they might tend to bring pressure on Her Majesty.

I became aware for the first time that it was at the Queen's special request that Lord Derby in 1866 requested Lord Clarendon to continue in the Foreign Office. In sending to Lord Derby at that time she stated he was the only person capable of forming an administration which would command 'her confidence and that of the country'.[2]

**274** 3 December 1868 *Conversation with General Grey: WEG's impressions of Grey*
ADD MS 44756 f 65

December 3. 1868.
This day I came up with General Grey and halt on my way to town for an audience with respect to the case of Clarendon.

We have had *fuller* communication than ever before upon all sorts of subjects touching the Crown and public affairs and he impressed me very favourably as to his devoted and scrupulous loyalty, and as to his intelligence and moderation in political opinions.

I found him a reformer in army matters: pacific in foreign affairs, with a colour a little too specifically German: but in all things having all the marks of a high integrity and no disposition to abuse his peculiar situation by playing the courtier.

He spoke with very great anxiety of *some* matters touching the Queen which he fears may lead to difficulty. They do not belong to political relations but might have political effects.[3]

---

[1] See preceding document.

[2] The Queen to Derby, 27 June 1866, George Earle Buckle, ed., *Letters of Queen Victoria*, Second series, 1926–1928, i. 342.

[3] On Windsor Castle notepaper. On f 66 are some pencilled notes by WEG which are practically illegible. For Grey's account of this conversation, see his memorandum of 4 December, *L.Q.V.*, 2nd series, i. 559–564.

**275**  3 December 1868   *Audience with the Queen: the new Ministry*
ADD MS 44756 ff 69–70

My first interview with Her Majesty was on Thursday [3 December]. Her Majesty began by asking me whether I had come prepared to accept the commission to form a new administration. My answer was, 'Madam, I have no choice: and I have only to regret that my powers whether of body or mind are not better suited for the purpose.'

We spent most of the time on the subject of the Foreign Office and Lord Clarendon, already opened to her by my letter to the Dean of Windsor,[1] and by General Grey. I pointed out the disadvantages of passing him over which Her Majesty appreciated: and I suggested a mode by which it appeared to me that without committing Her Majesty due caution could be given. Her Majesty stipulated that I should first try whether Clarendon would take any other office—as I had admitted Granville's admirable qualifications for the Foreign Office— and if he would not then he should be Foreign Secretary with the admonition which was to be considered common to him and to his colleagues.

I then submitted the names of Granville, Page Wood (Cockburn would have been very unacceptable), Cardwell, Childers, for the offices they finally took, and of Argyll for the President of the Council.

There was no allusion to the Irish Church. The Queen was kind, cheerful, even playful.

She heard from me that I had spoken to no one except Granville, Cardwell, and Clarendon—and she said she was by no means afraid of new men, in particular of Mr. Bright, who had several times spoken of her with great kindness; a thing which she always remembered and felt grateful for.[2]                                            *December 6.*

**276**  5 December 1868   *Further audience with the Queen: the new Ministry*
ADD MS 44756 ff 67–68

Yesterday I went through a long budget at Windsor with the Queen perfectly kind and accessible.

---

[1] Perhaps the letter of 29 November, ADD MS 44339, ff 56–60.

[2] For the Queen's account of this interview, see her memorandum of 3 December, *L.Q.V.*, 2nd series, i. 564–566.

She expressed her desire to have Lord Halifax but admitted there were difficulties and that others must be dealt with before him, as he had 'retired' and taken his peerage.

By Cardwell's particular desire, I, with questionable prudence, mentioned his anxiety to lay before her his views on a clause in the patent of Secretary for War which he considered (rightly I think) to interfere with parliamentary responsibility. I told her I believed his views were those of Sir James Graham. She said there was one clause of reservation in it which she considered of great importance.

I asked her whether I ought not to kiss hands: she said yes and it was done.

The Queen in agreeing to the offer to Lord Hartington referred to the Duchess of Manchester as 'another lady who must not do the honours'. I told Her Majesty that I thought ladies of his family would be found to discharge the duties of vice-reine.

The Queen adverted to various forms of Clarendon's rashness of speech: and had likewise the idea of some indelicacy.

The Queen adverted to the Irish Church—when the time for the train was fast approaching—and desired that some connection however slender with the Crown should be maintained. I simply expressed a hope that when the scurry was a little gone by Her Majesty would allow me a few minutes to present the subject from our point of view and said I did not despair of suggesting what might be in some degree consolatory to Her Majesty.                                    *December 6.*

*Extract from the Queen's journal, 5 December 1868*[1]

Saw Mr. Gladstone, who was, as the other day, most amiable. He spoke of the appointments that had been settled, and of those which were to be proposed, and I annex the list from his letter,[2] enumerating them, to save time. He told me about Mr. Bright, having at last consented 'after a terrible struggle'. That he had argued the matter with him from 10 to 12 last night. That Mr. Bright had not slept a wink all night. 'It is like taking a wild man of the woods and putting him into a court waistcoat.' That he accepted with reservations even as to dress, his stile belonging to the Society of Friends, though not conforming in speech and dress. For that reason he did not wish to be Secretary of

---

[1] The Royal Archives.
[2] Guedalla, i. no. 80.

State for India, or to have anything to do with peace or war. But he would go to the Board of Trade. He had been much gratified by what I had said of him. The offices of state were also talked over, and he was in great hopes the Duchess of Argyll would accept, only her health was not good. Talked of the arrangements respecting Parliament.

**277**  17–22 July 1869  *Negotiations on the Lords' amendments to the Irish Church Bill*[1]
ADD MS 44758 ff 1–14

*The following documents relate to the final stages of the Bill to disestablish the Church of Ireland. The disestablished Church was to be endowed with £500,000 for the support of its clergy, and the remainder of the funds arising from the sale of its property (the 'residue') was to be applied to welfare purposes in Ireland. Various amendments were introduced in the Lords. The government stood firm against 'concurrent endowment', or simultaneous endowment of the episcopalian, Roman Catholic and presbyterian bodies in Ireland; but, in order to avoid a constitutional struggle between Lords and Commons, they were prepared to concede an increase in the compensation secured to the disestablished Church and its clergy. The financial negotiations that followed are recorded in this memorandum and its attached papers. The Bill became law on 26 July 1869.*

Saturday, July 17.
On the 16th of July the amendments made by the Lords in the Irish Church Bill had been completely disposed of by the House of Commons.[2] The last division, taken on the disposal of the residue, had, chiefly through mere lazy absences, reduced the majority for the government to 72. This *relative* weakness offered a temptation to the opposition to make play upon the point.

The Cabinet met the next forenoon.[3] We felt on the one hand that it might be difficult to stake the Bill on the clause for the disposal of the residue, supposing that to be the single remaining point of difference: but that the postponement of this question would be a greater moral

---

[1] In WEG's hand. WEG left spaces in the text for the insertion of copies of documents which he indicated by letters. These copies are in a secretary's hand.

[2] For these amendments, see WEG's speech of 15 July (*Parliamentary Debates*, 3rd series, cxcvii. 1891–1892).

[3] WEG's notes of this Cabinet meeting: ADD MS 44637, f 83.

and political evil, and that any concession made by us had far better be one which would be of some value to the disestablished Church.

We thought the Archbishop of Canterbury would probably enter into this view: and that without committing the Queen to any particular recommendation, she might be disposed again to move him in the sense of peace.

By desire of the Cabinet I went to Windsor in the afternoon,[1] and represented to Her Majesty what it was in our power to do: namely, although we had done all we could upon the merits, yet, for the sake of peace and of the House of Lords:

(a) to make some one further pecuniary concession to the Church of sensible though not very large amount;
(b) to make a further concession as to curates, slight in itself;
(c) to amend the residue clause so as to give to Parliament the future controul, and to be content with simply declaring the principle on which the property should be distributed.

The Queen while considering that she could not be a party to this or that particular scheme, agreed that it might be proper to make a representation to the Archbishop to the general effect that the views of the government at this crisis of the measure were such as deserved to be weighed, and to promote confidential communication between us. She intimated her intention to employ the Dean of Windsor as a medium of communication between herself and the Archbishop, and wished me to explain particulars fully to him.

I went to the deanery and not finding the Dean, had written as much as here follows on a scrap of paper, when he came in:[2]

The desire of the Archbishop and bishops generally is supposed to be to secure the greatest amount of property to the Church.

While this was hoped for by means of concurrent endowment, and concurrent endowment by means of the postponement of the surplus, the postponement was an object to the Archbishop, the episcopal bench, and many likeminded lay peers.

The clause for concurrent endowment was condemned in the House of Commons *without a division*, and the House of Commons has reinstated in the preamble, and will unquestionably maintain

---

[1] The Queen's account of this audience: *L.Q.V.*, 2nd series, ii. 618.
[2] Document 'A'. The original is ADD MS 44757, f 150.

there at whatever hazard the words which exclude any appropriation of the surplus to religious uses.

It does not therefore appear what interest the bishops and other peers abovenamed can now feel in the postponement.

The government are still in a position in which it might be possible to make some small further concession in point of temporalities to the Church: but if the postponement of the surplus be insisted on by the Lords, this would be wholly out of the question.

The object of this paper was to incline the Archbishop to discountenance any plan for pressing the postponement of the provisions respecting the residue, and to deal with us in preference respecting any practicable concession to the Church.

When the Dean came in I explained this further, recited the purport of my interview with the Queen, and on his asking me confidentially for his own information let him know that the further pecuniary concession we were prepared to recommend would be some £170,000 or £180,000, and that this if applied to encourage commutation would be of much more value to the Church than the same amount given in another way.

He proposed to see the Archbishop early on Monday.

Sunday, July 18.
In the afternoon Lord Granville called on me and brought to me a confidential memorandum, containing an overture, which Mr. Disraeli had placed in the hands of Lord Bessborough for communication to us. He had represented the terms as those which he had with much difficulty induced Lord Cairns to consent to. This was the memorandum.[1]

While the contention as to the residue was here abandoned, and pecuniary concessions alone were sought, the demand amounted, according to our computation, to between £900,000 and £1,000,000.

We discussed the matter at much length. The amendments of the

---

[1] Document 'B'. Not inserted. There is a note in pencil at this point: 'In a letter to Lord Granville, September 3 '69, Mr. G. says: "Bessborough cannot find B." ' See Agatha Ramm, ed., *The Political Correspondence of Mr. Gladstone and Lord Granville 1868–1876*, Royal Historical Society, Camden series, lxxxi, lxxxii, 1952, no. 120. For calculations of the financial value of the concessions made and demanded see ADD MS 44757, ff 148–149, 151.

Lords had originally according to our computation given nearly £2,800,000 to the Church besides some £1,100,000 as its share of the concurrent endowment. In the Commons we had conceded £780,000. The new demands raised this (say) to £1,750,000 or nearly two-thirds of the matter in dispute. This it was evident was utterly inadmissible. I saw no possibility of approach to it: and considered that a further quarter of a million or thereabouts was all which the House of Commons could be expected or asked further to concede. On the same afternoon Lord Granville, falling in with Mr. Goschen, asked him what he thought the very most that could be had—would it be £500,000? Goschen answered £300,000 and with this Glyn agreed.

Mr. Disraeli desired an answer before three on Monday.[1]

Monday, July 19.
Those members of the government who had acted as a sort of committee in the Irish Church question met in the afternoon.[2]

We were all agreed in opinion that the Disraeli overture must be rejected though without closing the door: and a reply was prepared in this sense which Lord Granville undertook to send as follows:[3]

Draft. July 19. 1869.
The government have already (in their own judgment) now strained every point in favour of the Church as far as the merits are concerned.

All that remains is to say to the majority of the House of Commons *such and such a sum* is not worth the quarrel and the postponement.

This sum must be moderate.

The sum asked is according to estimate of the government between £900,000 and a million.

No such sum or any sum approaching it, could be asked of the majority.

Meantime the Archbishop had arrived in Downing Street, in pursuance of the arrangements of Saturday: and a paper was either now drawn, or sanctioned by my colleagues, I do not remember which, in order to

---

[1] See also WEG to Granville, 18 July, ibid., no. 89.

[2] Here are the following words, afterwards deleted: 'The Archbishop of Canterbury had previously come to me from Lord Cairns with a memorandum in which he proposed as the basis of a settlement.'

[3] Document 'C'. The original is ADD MS 44757, f 152.

form the basis of my communication to the Archbishop. I here append it.[1]

Points not yet settled.

1. 'Postponement' (absolute). This, if urged, puts out of the question all the rest.
   If not urged, let us go on.
2. Date. May be freely yielded, if *House of Lords desire it.*
3. Commutation clause. Lords' clause cannot work: is a dead letter. Ours is preferred by the Church.
4. Glebe houses. Concession on this is now become impossible, from the close and palpable relation into which the subject has now come with 'concurrent endowment'.
5. Tax. An amendment most impolitic for the Church, as it will enable every congregation to throw on the central fund the expenses of its own worship.
6. Ulster glebes. Any one may judge for himself whether any charmer could charm the House of Commons on this subject?
   Also the joint claim of the Presbyterians has been admitted by some on the Conservative side.
7. Deduction of curates' stipends. On this if it stood alone, a further concession might be possible, *simply as an act of deference to the House of Lords:* e.g. *half-deduction.*
   But supposing the discussion to have reached this point the question plainly arises whether, presuming a certain further amount of money is to be given, this particular *mode* of giving it is the best.
   On this point, if solitary, there would be no difficulty in arriving at an understanding. *July 19. 1869.*

I returned from my interview with the Archbishop, and reported, as I afterwards did to the Dean of Windsor, that his tone was friendly, and that he appeared well disposed to the sort of arrangement I had sketched.[2]

Tuesday, July 20.
The Archbishop, who had communicated with Lord Cairns in the interval, came to me early today and brought a memorandum as a

---

[1] Document 'D'. The original in WEG's hand is ADD MS 44756, ff 30–31.
[2] See also WEG to the Queen, 19 July, *L.Q.V.*, 2nd series, ii. 618–619.

basis of agreement, which to my surprise, demanded higher terms than those of Mr. Disraeli.

| | |
|---|---|
| 1. The Lords amendment as to curates to be adopted | 380,000 |
| 2. The Ulster glebes | 465,000 |
| 3. The glebe houses to be free | 150,000 |
| | 995,000 |

or, the Bishop of Peterborough's amendment as to the tax upon livings in lieu of no. 3 would carry a heavier charge by                    124,000

making 1,119,000

I told the Archbishop the terms in which we had already expressed ourselves to Mr. Disraeli. The Archbishop saw me again in the afternoon, but had no more to say than that he did not mean to ask for more than Mr. Disraeli had asked. I told the Archbishop—whether today or yesterday I am not sure, but today if not yesterday, the nature and value of the pecuniary concession we were prepared to make, placing it at near £300,000. This however was for himself alone in strict confidence.

Meantime an answer had come from Mr. Disraeli stating that he could do no more.[1]

Then followed the meeting of the opposition peers at the Duke of Marlborough's.

On the meeting of the Houses, a few of us considered what course was to be taken if the Lords should again cast out of the preamble the words which precluded concurrent endowment: and it was agreed to stay the proceedings for the time, and consider among ourselves what further to do.[2] Lord Granville made this announcement accordingly after the Lords had upon a hot debate and by a large majority excluded our words from the preamble. This had been after a speech from Lord Cairns, in which he announced his intention of moving other amendments which he detailed and which were in general conformable to the proposals already made to us.

The first disposition of several of us this evening myself included was

---

[1] Document 'E'. 'E' deleted in pencil, and the document not inserted.

[2] Note in pencil by Granville in the margin: 'The first order I received was to throw up the Bill, to which I answered that I could not do more than adjourn the debate. G.'

to regard the proceeding of the opposition as now complete: since the whole had been announced, the first stroke struck, and the command shown of a force of peers amply sufficient to do the rest. The reports also were that this was expected and desired by the House of Commons. And I for one had no doubt that the issue thus joined before the country would be intelligible and that we should completely succeed. The idea did not however include an absolute abandonment of the Bill but only the suspension of our responsibility for it, leaving the opposition to work their own will, and with the intention, when this had been done of considering the matter further.

Here I insert a passage from Lord Granville:

'On the return of the amendments to the House of Lords, in answer to my question, "I presume you have nothing to say to me?" Lord Cairns said "No".'

Wednesday, July 21.
The Cabinet met at 11:[1] and I went to it in the mind of last night. We discussed however at great length all possible methods of proceeding which occurred to us. The result was stated in a letter of mine to the Queen of which I annex a copy:[2]

Mr. Gladstone presents his humble duty to Your Majesty and reports that the Cabinet met at 11 this day, and considered with anxious care its position and duty in regard to the Irish Church Bill. The vote and declarations of the House of Lords last night were regarded as fatal if persisted in; and the Cabinet deemed it impossible to meet proceedings of such a character with any tender of further concessions.

The Cabinet however considered at much length a variety of courses; as
(1) to announce at once that they could no longer, after the vote and announcements of last night be responsible for further proceedings in connection with the Bill, but that they would leave it to the majority of the House of Lords to take such steps as it might think proper;
(2) to go through the whole of the amendments on the Bill, and then, if they were adversely carried, to declare and proceed as above;

[1] WEG's notes of this meeting: ADD MS 44637, ff 90–91.
[2] Document 'F'.

12

(3) to go through not the whole of the amendments, but the endowment amendments and to conclude that when these had been adversely decided, they could (as before) assume no further responsibility, but must leave the matter to the majority to consider;

(4) to send the Bill back to the House of Commons, with the declaration that it would not be accepted there, and with the intention of simply moving the House to adhere to its amendments as last adjusted.

Your Majesty has already been apprised by Mr. Gladstone's telegram in cipher of this afternoon, that (under the influence of a strong desire to exhibit patience, and to leave open every opportunity for reconsideration) the third of these courses had been adopted; although there was no doubt that the House of Commons was fully prepared to approve and sustain the first. Lord Granville deemed it just possible, that the peers might be prepared to give way upon another return of the Bill from the House of Commons: and the question therefore was left open whether, if evidence to this effect should appear, the government should then fall in with that course of proceeding.

Although the government have felt it to be impossible to make biddings in the face of the opposition, the Archbishop of Canterbury has been apprised, in strict confidence, of the nature and extent of the concession, which for the sake of peace they would be prepared to recommend.

Sir R. Palmer is also substantially aware of it and has expressed his opinion that on such terms the opposition ought to be ready to conclude the matter.

11 Carlton House Terrace
21 July 1869.

Most of the Cabinet were desirous to go on longer: others, myself included, objected to proceeding to the end of the Bill (plan    )[1] or undertaking to remit the Bill again to the House of Commons as of our own motion. It occurred to me however that we might proceed as far as to the end of the money amendments, about the middle of the Bill: and this appeared to meet the views of all, even of those who would have preferred doing more, or less.

---

[1] Blank in MS. Should be: 'plan 2'.

Thursday, July 22.

I was laid up today and the transactions were carried on by Lord Granville, in communication with me from time to time at my house.

First he brought me a note he had received from Lord Cairns.[1]

Private and confidential                              5, Cromwell House
                                                      22 July 1869

My dear Lord Granville,

I have no right and no desire to ask for any information as to the course which you propose to take tonight: but if the statements as to the intention of the government to proceed with the consideration of the amendments be correct, and if you think that any advantage can result from it, you will find me ready, as you know I have throughout been, to confer upon a mode—and I think a mode can be suggested—by which without sacrifice of principle or dignity upon either side the remaining points of difference might be arranged.

I leave this on my way to the bankruptcy committee, House of Lords. I could see you if you wish it either at the Colonial Office, or at your own house.

Yours very truly,

(signed) Cairns

He then saw Lord Cairns and obtained his terms. They were somewhat but not very greatly improved. The Ulster glebes however were gone. He now demanded

(1) the acceptance of the amendment respecting curates        380,000
(2) five per cent to be added to the seven per cent on
    commutations                                             300,000
(3) the glebe houses to be given to the Church at ten years
    purchase of the sites: in truth a slight modification of
    the amendment of Lord Salisbury say                      140,000

I think these three heads were stated in a memorandum of Lord Cairns's.[2] I attach to each of these the money value he put upon them: and it appears that even in the mid hours of this final day Lord Cairns asked above £800,000.

---

[1] Document 'G'.

[2] This sentence was added afterwards in the margin.

We held our ground and declared we could on special grounds accede to the second amendment if that were accepted as sufficient: but not to the first nor the third. We offered however to reduce the 68th clause to a simple legislative declaration, which in truth was from the first in our view the essence of it, but it had been inflamed and magnified by their suspicions. And we offered to meet an objection rightly taken by Lord Cairns on a point of detail with respect to the proof of the 'permanent' character of a curate, where our provision was not sufficient for its end.

In a second interview with Lord Granville, Lord Cairns gave up the proposal relating to glebe houses.

In a third, at which the Attorney-General for Ireland was present, the substance of the demand as to curates was given up: and it was agreed on our part that the curate should be charged on the incumbent not when a deduction for salary had been allowed during the one year specified, but during a term of five years.

It was now 4.30 when Lord Cairns with much courage undertook to propose to his party acquiescence in these terms.

There was another change pressed by and conceded to him, which I have not yet mentioned. The $(7+5=)$ 12 per cent were to be added to the commutation money when three-quarters instead of four-fifths of the annuitants had expressed their readiness to commute. This change tends to diminish the number of *commutants*, and thus positively to diminish, probably or possibly by some 30,000 or 35,000 the pecuniary value of the concession we had tendered.[1]

The news was brought to me on my sofa and between 5 and 6 I was enabled to telegraph to the Queen.

My telegram was followed up by a letter at 7 p.m. which announced that the arrangement had been accepted by the House of Lords, and that a general satisfaction prevailed.[2]

Mr. Gladstone presents his humble duty to Your Majesty, and reports that, after a long and anxious day of communications carried

---

[1] There is a note in pencil at this point: 'Take in H'. Document 'H' has not been found.

[2] Document 'I'. Not inserted in the text. Transcribed from the original in the Royal Archives, D26/103.

on between Lord Granville and Lord Cairns, he was enabled to telegraph to Your Majesty this evening in cipher as follows:

'The points in dispute on the Irish Church Bill have been settled between the government and the leader of the opposition, and both Houses will be recommended to adopt the measure.'

Mr. Gladstone is at a loss to account for the great change in the tone and views of the opposition since Sunday, and Monday, and even Tuesday last; but on this topic it is needless to enter.

As to the principal matters, the basis of the arrangement on the side of the government is much the same, as was intended when Mr. Gladstone had the honour of an audience at Windsor on Saturday; but various minor concessions have been added.

Mr. Gladstone does not doubt that, if the majority of the House of Lords shall accede to the advice of Lord Cairns, the government will be able to induce the House of Commons to agree to the conditions proposed.

Mr. Gladstone would in vain strive to express to Your Majesty the relief, thankfulness, and satisfaction, with which he contemplates not only the probable passing of what many believe to be a beneficent and necessary measure, but the undoubted and signal blessing of an escape from a formidable constitutional conflict.

The skill, patience, assiduity, and sagacity, of Lord Granville in the work of today demand from Mr. Gladstone the tribute of his warm admiration.

Though Parliament is sitting, a slight indisposition, which has confined Mr. Gladstone during the day, obliges him to address Your Majesty from his own house.

Mr. Gladstone has just had the honour to receive Your Majesty's letter of this day:[1] to which the foregoing statement will have afforded his best reply.

PS. At the last moment Mr. Gladstone learns that the House of Lords agrees, and that a general satisfaction prevails.[2]

11 Carlton House Terrace

July 22. 1869. 7.00 p.m.

*August 14. 1869.*

---

[1] *L.Q.V.*, 2nd series, ii. 620–621.

[2] The Queen's reply: ibid., ii. 622.

**278** 25 June 1871 *Conversation with the Queen: a royal residence in Ireland*[1]

ADD MS 44760 ff 40–45[2]

*Most private.*

I have had a long and interesting conversation with the Queen today on the subject of 'Royal Residence in Ireland'.

She began with some apparent disinclination to the subject, was disposed to disparage Ireland and the Irish; said so much had been done for them already, more than for Scotland or for England; and threw out the opinion that, though there might be occasional visits of one or another member of the Royal Family, yet, if any thing more or more systematic were attempted, it would lead to false hopes, exactions, and other inconveniences. She quoted Lord Dufferin once or twice as leaning more or less towards her views of Ireland: and thought want of personal security was a serious impediment to royal visits on any considerable scale.

I first opened the 'minor plan', of a royal residence, to be provided by parliamentary vote, with a grant to meet some portion of the expence of living there. I stated that I had nothing of a definite character to propose on the part of the Cabinet; but I described what had taken place during the last few years in Parliament with reference to the question, and how it had grown at length into the shape of a regular notice of motion on which a good deal of interest appeared to be concentrated. I pointed out that the subject had been touched generally both by the late and the present government, as one not unworthy to be entertained: and I repeatedly pressed upon this consideration that it was to be regarded by no means as an exclusively Irish question, but as likely to be of great utility in strengthening the Throne under circumstances which require all that can be done in that sense, if indeed we can make it a new means of putting forward the Royal Family in the visible discharge of public duty. The desirableness and necessity of any plan likely to have this effect the Queen readily admitted. The plan, however, did not seem to find favour with her, and especially she anticipated me in declaring rather positively that it would not do

---

[1] The subject of a royal residence in Ireland was discussed by the Cabinet on 24 June (ADD MS 44639, f 67).

[2] On Windsor Castle notepaper. ADD MS 44760, ff 46–50 is a copy of this document in secretary's hand.

for the Prince of Wales. She mentioned considerations of health, of time, of character; was afraid of his being identified with Ireland, of his being surrounded with flatterers, and was doubtful of his disposition to act steadily upon any plan that might be laid down, and other matters.

I quoted with some emphasis the opinions of Lord Spencer and Lord Bessborough with reference to a plan of this kind, and I pleaded much in favour of the Prince of Wales; dwelling on the difficulties of his position, which he might have been better able to encounter if he had been endowed with the gifts and character of his father, but which it really was hard for any commoner man to cope with. I contended that, if duty were found for him, he might show or acquire a disposition to do it. I admitted that, if anything serious were to be undertaken, it must be the subject of a regular understanding with him, and that the continuance of the arrangement with him must depend upon the manner in which he might set about its execution. She contended that he would not like it. This however was in the next stage of the conversation.

I pressed a good deal the general gravity of the subject, while speaking for the most part in my own name and only referring occasionally to the government, in order to avoid giving too definitive a character to the discussion, and to use it as a means of ascertaining in what direction it was best to move; I referred to the fact that there were various modes of proceeding: and she, giving way a little, began to entertain the matter more favourably, and said that it had been once recommended to her, by some person, that Prince Arthur should go to Ireland as Lord Lieutenant.

This gave me an excellent opportunity of opening the larger scheme, as the small one had had all the fair play I could obtain for it, and had not been very successful. Without giving up the case for the Prince of Wales, I now said that of course any member of the Royal Family going to Dublin to represent Her Majesty must stand wholly detached from the ministry of the day and from political responsibility. But she thought he ought to be kept cognisant of business, and should have the opportunity of forming and giving opinions on it confidentially: so that in fact I found Her Majesty at this point quite on the same line of thought with myself. However, without dwelling very specially upon this part of the case, we pursued the subject generally from the more extended point of view. I referred to what had taken place under the government of Lord Russell, and observed that the Irish department must be reconstituted, and a Cabinet minister of well defined station and attributes appointed to discharge with adequate authority the administrative duties of the Lord Lieutenant. She said that liberal time must be allowed for visits and duties in this country, but did not think four or even six months too much to contemplate as the portion of the year to be given to Ireland. It was in dealing with this part of the case that when she said the Prince of Wales would not like it, I pointed out that he would receive, by a plan of this kind, an assistance to his income which might be acceptable.

In fact, though it was all dragging, so to speak, while we were on the smaller plan, the Queen talked with content and freedom and a good deal of approval of the abolition of the Lord Lieutenancy, and the substitution of a royal representation of the Sovereign. The whole matter seemed to have become congenial to her. But I was careful to explain that though it would probably be my duty to report something very shortly, from the Cabinet, of a more substantive character, I did not seek to commit her to anything now said but merely to break ground upon the case.

As the conversation went on, two circumstances happened which gave it a more favourable turn with respect also to the Prince of Wales. First it occurred to her, that residence in Dublin, and duties assumed there, might interfere with the military career of Prince Arthur. And secondly, she said she should like to speak in great confidence to one or two persons: to Sir Thomas Biddulph and perhaps to the Dean of Windsor. I told her I had already conversed with the Dean: and had found him very much impressed with the advantages of the plan and particularly in reference to the Prince of Wales. Whether from these or other causes I know not, but undoubtedly the Queen very much relented on this, the point with respect to which she had been stiff, and ended with freely allowing that it was a fair subject for consideration. The upshot of the whole conversation then was, as to the smaller plan, adverse; she said it would not work: as to the larger plan, decidedly favourable: as to the Prince of Wales, quite open.

The Queen entirely agreed that, if a scheme of this kind were to be adopted, the execution should follow promptly on the announcement, and that the proper time would be the opening of the next session.

*June 25. 1871.*[1]

---

[1] See WEG to Granville, 26 June, enclosing a copy of this memorandum. 'Shall I circulate it to the Cabinet or only to those who were first spoken to?' Ramm (1868–1871), no. 539. Granville's reply is not known.

*Memorandum by the Queen, 25 June*[1]

Mr. Gladstone spoke to me on the subject of *Ireland* this afternoon, and on the wish expressed again and again that there should be a royal residence there, and said that a *motion* on the subject was about to be brought on, to which an answer must be given. We went over the old ground, the unnecessary pretensions of the Irish to have more done for them than the Welsh or English; the visits to Scotland being in *no one way political* or connected with the wishes of the people, but *merely* because the climate and scenery are so healthy and beautiful, and the people so charming, so loyal, and the residence there of the greatest possible advantage (to mind and body) to our family, myself, and *everyone* connected with me and my household. That, therefore, to press and urge this was unreasonable.

To have a residence in Ireland, and *not* go there, would be *worse*, and that *occasional* visits would be better, and that they must depend on the state of the country.

Mr. Gladstone contended how important it was in *these days* to connect the *Royal Family* with *public functions* and *offices*, and that it would be very important to do this *in Ireland*. I contended that it would be wasting time in *spending* this *in Ireland*, when Scotland and England deserved it much more. Mr. Gladstone, however, thought it would be *a great* advantage, and mentioned Lord Spencer and Lord Bessborough as being strongly of opinion *what* good it would do, if *someone* of the family were *frequently* to go there for a short time.

If there was to be a residence it would entail someone of the family going there for a short while *every year*. I pointed out the great difficulty of this—the sacrifice and tax it would be to anyone, considering their various other duties, and residences, etc. He mentioned the Prince of Wales and I resisted this, saying it would only make him still more unsettled, would identify him too much with Ireland and he would have no time to do it, nor would he do it; and that I feared from his habits of amusement and excitement that it would do more harm than good. To this Mr. Gladstone replied that *that must* be made a condition and that he must be made to understand that he could *not* undertake anything of the kind if he did *not fulfil* the conditions *required*.

---

[1] The Royal Archives, D27/74. Printed with omissions in *L.Q.V.*, 2nd series, ii. 136–138.

I urged that Arthur would be much fitter for such a position for *his* steadiness, tact and conciliatoriness. But I then observed that it struck me that, *if* such an idea were entertained, the notion which had been entertained by several people of making a royal prince Lord Lieutenant would be *far* the *best*. Mr. Gladstone said he thought I was right, and that this *was* the *better* and easier plan of *the two*. Of course a *royal prince* could *not* be *responsible*, and the *Secretary for Ireland* must be made an *important responsible minister*. But that to have a *non*-political Lord Lieutenant would be far better, and that it certainly would be far easier to do this than to have a mere occasional residence there *without any* ostensible *object*. Arthur I thought particularly suited for this; only he could not be banished there for ever, as I should want him to be with me. Five or six months in the course of the year would be quite enough, Mr. Gladstone said, and that all that could easily be managed. I added that I did not know, however, how this might do with Arthur's career as a soldier, and probably could not be for long, and that at any rate I must speak to Colonel Elphinstone before I could say anything more on the subject.

We then talked over the possibility of the Prince of Wales doing this, though I doubted the wisdom of identifying the future king with Ireland, and depriving him of his own home, and of going to Scotland, both of which were important for his health, Ireland having a bad climate. In this case, Mr. Gladstone said, three or four months would be quite enough. If it could take him more away from the London season I said it would be a good thing, but not if it took him away from the country, and from Scotland, where I saw most of him. It *would* take him away more from London, Mr. Gladstone said, and he thinks it would give him something to do, and check the life of idle dissipation which does so much harm.

I said I must think it well over before I could make up my mind as to the best course to pursue. Mr. Gladstone thanked me very much, and said he would await my answer, but wished it to be kept very secret. I said that Arthur had been mentioned to me by several people as *fit* for this post.[1]

---

[1] The subject was discussed by the Cabinet again on 1 and 5 July (ADD MS 44369, ff 68, 70). See Guedalla, i. nos. 351, 352, for WEG's report of the Cabinet meeting of 5 July, and the Queen's discouraging reply.

**279** 21 December 1871 *Conversation with the Queen: service of thanksgiving for the recovery of the Prince of Wales*
ADD MS 44760 ff 129–136

*On 19 November 1871 the Prince of Wales was taken ill with typhoid fever, the disease from which his father had died; and for some weeks his condition was critical. On his recovery, WEG suggested a public thanksgiving service in St. Paul's Cathedral. He wrote to Granville on 22 December: 'I was with the Queen yesterday for an hour. No one can be a worse reporter than I am of conversations; but I have put down some notes of this. I inclose the paper and beg you to return it. It will look as if written to show that I produced a considerable effect on the Queen's mind. But probably she had made it up to the effect of starting with very strong doctrine, so as to be able to part with some of it on the way.'*[1]

Windsor. December 21. 1871.
The Queen received a letter yesterday from Lord Halifax, in which he expressed pleasure at hearing that she had agreed to go in state to St. Paul's to return thanks for the recovery (on its being completed or sufficiently advanced) of the Prince of Wales.[2] Of this I heard on reaching Windsor yesterday: and I learned that it had much discomposed the Queen. She had, upon the occasion thus given, written a letter to Colonel Ponsonby, in which she very clearly and succinctly separated three subjects. First, some communication, by which she should make known to the country her warm sense of the sympathy and loyalty shown during the illness. Secondly, a form of thanksgiving to be used in public worship throughout the country. Thirdly this idea of a procession to St. Paul's: on which she did not, in the letter, put an absolute negative, but she treated it as something ulterior and contingent, to be considered separately, if at all, on its own merits.

I told the Queen her view of the case had been communicated to me and I entirely concurred in it. It was then decided by Her Majesty to write to me a letter, in which she should express her own feelings for herself, about the manifestation of sympathy by the people: this I am to send to Bruce as Home Secretary for publication.[3] As respects the

---

[1] Ramm (1871–1876), no. 617.

[2] See Halifax to WEG, 22 December, WEG to Halifax, 23 December; ADD MS 44185, ff 239–241.

[3] For the Queen's letter, 26 December, see Guedalla, i. no. 408, and *The Times*, 30 December.

form of thanksgiving, I said Sir W. Jenner had informed me that Dr. Gull and he could not as yet speak of any particular interval, after which convalescence might be reasonably anticipated, and until they had done so, it seemed plain that nothing could be said. I was then proceeding to introduce the other subject, that of going solemnly to St. Paul's, when the Queen delivered a very strong declaration against it. She objected to it because she disliked in an extreme degree the cathedral service. She objected still more because she thought such a display, in point of religion, false and hollow. She considered that no religious act ought ever to be allied with pomp or show. Nothing should induce her to be a party to it. It would be of no use to press her as this was her conviction with regard to the religious part of the subject.

I first tried the point of time, and said that there could be no occasion to press Her Majesty at present, as it would be premature. But she said it was no question of time with her; that she wished now to deal with it once for all, and that she hoped I would never return to the subject.

Then I fell back on the Princess of Wales, and said I had understood she was very desirous that there should be a public and solemn act of this kind by which to render thanks; and I could not help thinking that very probably the Prince of Wales would share this feeling. I said it would be very difficult to refuse to him and to her, the gratification of such a wish. The Queen replied she did not think the Princess of Wales would now press it so much, after what she (the Queen) had said to her.

'Well, Madam,' I said, 'I grant all that Your Majesty had urged with reference to the nature of these ceremonials, if they are to be considered merely as vehicles for the expression of the religious feelings of those who are to be the principal actors in them. But in the first place I feel convinced that there will be a very general desire expressed for something of this character, and if done it will give universal satisfaction. The sympathy of the country has gone beyond precedent—and beyond description: feeling has been wrought up to the highest point, and nothing short of a great public act of this kind can form an adequate answer to it. But besides this, Madam, let it be considered if you please whether Your Majesty or those who are to appear as principal personages may not properly cast aside all thought of themselves; and their own feelings, in the matter: it may be most unsatisfactory to them individually, but ought we not to remember the great religious importance of such an act for the people at large: on them it will make a deep impression—it will be a signal honour done to religion in their view.

23

There are in these times but few occasions on which great national acts of religion can be performed; and this appears to be one of them, for which the opportunity has now been offered.'

These considerations appeared to tell very much with the Queen. I then dwelt upon the extreme solemnity of the occasion: not only for the Prince, as any one after such an illness must be decidedly a better or a worse man for it, and not only for the Queen and Royal Family, but for the future of the monarchy and of the country as connected with it. It had worked in an extraordinary manner to the effect of putting down that disagreeable movement with which the name of Sir C. Dilke had been connected. And what we should look to I thought was not merely meeting that movement by a more powerful display of opposite opinion, but to getting rid of it altogether, for it never could be satisfactory that there should exist even a fraction of the nation republican in its views. To do this it would be requisite to consider every mode in which this great occasion could be turned to account, and if possible to take away the causes which had led to the late manifestations.

The Queen urged that the state of things in France had had much to do with them and that in 1848 the case was worse.

I admitted both but said that since 1848 the foundation of the movement of that date had been broken up and all tendencies of that kind pretty well got rid of: also that it was to be feared that France might continue for a long time to be a source of sympathetic excitement, mischievously disturbing this country. I glanced at the necessity of finding for the Prince of Wales some means of living worthily of his great position and greater prospects: but this brought out no direct response: only there was a hope expressed by the Queen in some part of the conversation that the illness, and the display of feeling, would act directly in a beneficial manner on the Prince's character and conduct.

The latter part of the conversation turned more upon details: the Queen urging in turn all the difficulties. The uncertainty whether the Prince's health might allow him to take part, until the season was far advanced, when the ceremony would have lost all meaning. Then she said it would be more convenient and appropriate at Westminster Abbey where they were crowned. I said it was bad to go against the established tradition, as it provoked adverse remark: such for instance would be the case if a Sovereign desired to be crowned at St. Paul's. At length the Queen contracted her objection to the length of the service: and here I was able entirely to agree that the whole proceeding would have to be shortened. I referred Her Majesty to the *Annual Register* of 1789 (from which it appears that the Commons set out at 8 a.m.; the King and Queen at 10, and their Majesties only returned to the palace at half-past three).

When the objection was at the highest, I observed to the Queen that there were various modes in which if she were able to take part her participation might be arranged and reminded her of her appearance at Windsor on the occasions of royal marriages in St. George's Chapel.

I also told her in the course of arguing for the proposal that I admitted its religious importance was that of a symbol, but it was not therefore to be accounted slight: royalty was in one point of view a symbol, and one of great consequence: its character and duties had greatly changed among us in modern times, but perhaps in the new forms they were not less important than in the old.

At one time we got upon the topic of the lowered tone of society in the highest rank. This is a question the Queen has repeatedly opened to me: and I took the opportunity today of admitting the fact, and of observing that it was the active influence of the Court on that particular circle which had done so much to elevate and purify its tone during the earlier part of the reign. The Queen replied that they had observed this lowering process at work before the Prince's death, and that he was accustomed to attribute it to the augmented intercourse with France.

At one moment she started the idea that a Day of Thanksgiving might be appointed to be observed as a general holiday. I remarked that this would be viewed by many as an actual hardship, and by many more as involving something like a character of compulsion. Whereas if the procession to St. Paul's set the example while the day would be very much kept, I thought, all the observance would have the grace of being entirely voluntary.

The upshot of the whole was that the Queen is in no way committed, and that the whole idea is subject to considerations of health, but it is entertained, and not unfavourably. At one time the Queen said the Prince and Princess might go without her: but she did not dwell on this and I think saw that it would not do very well. *Christmas Day. 1871.*

*The Queen's account of this conversation in her journal :*[1]
Directly after luncheon saw Mr. Gladstone, who spoke very feelingly

---

[1] *L.Q.V.*, 2nd series, ii. 181. For further discussion between WEG and Granville, see Ramm (1871–1876), nos. 619–622.

about dear Bertie's illness, his present condition, and the wonderful feeling and sympathy which had been evinced on this occasion. I consulted Mr. Gladstone as to what could be done to express my sense of gratitude. After some discussion it was agreed that I should write him a letter, expressive of my deep feeling of the sympathy and loyalty shown.

**280**   12–16 March 1873   *Resignation and resumption of office*
ADD MS 44761 ff 100–101

*On the night of 11–12 March 1873 WEG's ministry was defeated on the second reading of the Irish University Bill. After two Cabinet meetings, and two audiences at which WEG explained the situation to the Queen, ministers resigned on 13 March. However, having established that Disraeli was determined not to attempt the formation of a Conservative ministry, WEG agreed on 16 March to re-form his government, and by 18 March he could tell the Queen that the entire Cabinet was ready to resume office.*

*On the evening of Thursday 13 March WEG recorded the events of the preceding few hours (VI below), and late on Sunday 16 March he noted the 'landmarks of the present crisis' (below). Also printed below are his summaries of the Cabinet meetings of 12 and 13 March (II and IV) and the Queen's own record of her interviews with him (I, III, V and VII).*

The landmarks of the present crisis are as follows.

On Wednesday morning [12 March] 2.45 a.m. I apprise the Queen of our defeat.[1]

In Cabinet at one we discuss the matter with a general tendency to resignation rather than dissolving.[2]

Before and after I see Her Majesty to keep her informed.[3]

Thursday [13 March] at noon the Cabinet determines to resign.[4]

---

[1] Guedalla, i. no. 518. Guedalla prints most of the correspondence of WEG, the Queen, Ponsonby and Disraeli on this matter between 12 and 18 March.

[2] See II, below.

[3] See I and III, below.

[4] See IV, below.

At 2.45 I apprise the Queen who accepts (and forthwith sends for Mr. Disraeli). I leave Her Majesty at 3.30.[1]

At 4.30 I apprise the House of Commons which adjourns until Monday.

Between 6 and 7 Colonel Ponsonby calls upon me to tell me from Her Majesty that Mr. Disraeli has been seen and has declined: and to ask advice.

I advise that Mr. Disraeli's answer be asked for in writing.[2]

On Friday [14 March] at 9 Colonel Ponsonby sends me Mr. Disraeli's answer in writing,[3] and calls at ten.

Upon examination afterwards I find the paper somewhat ambiguous, and write to Her Majesty hoping it will be cleared up.[4]

Between 6 and 7 I learn from Her Majesty (and Colonel Ponsonby again calls) that Mr. Disraeli's answer is an unconditional refusal: and asks for my advice.

I reply that the opposition could not acquit itself of its duty in the matter either by a previous determination to refuse or by a summary refusal without consultation upon the facts: and undertake to state fully my views in writing.

I take my statement (prepared after dinner) to Lord Granville's that night.

On Saturday morning [15 March] I see Lord Granville and Colonel Ponsonby: copy out and send off the statement:[5] I see Her Majesty at 2.45[6] when I learn that Mr. Disraeli did at his interview state that if I declined to resume he would then be at Her Majesty's command. I said to Her Majesty 'But that fact is not before me' (i.e. not in writing). 'But he said it to me', she replied.

My statement or part of it was sent by Her Majesty to Mr. Disraeli; no doubt before she started for Windsor at 4.30.

We went off to Cliveden.

On Sunday [16 March] at 10 p.m. a messenger reached Cliveden with a fresh summons to me from the Queen to say whether I will resume office.

---

[1] See V, below.

[2] See VI, below.

[3] Monypenny and Buckle, *Life of Disraeli*, v. 212.

[4] Guedalla, i. no. 524.

[5] Ibid., no. 526.

[6] See VII, below.

She incloses Mr. Disraeli's letter which shows nothing more is to be expected in that quarter.[1]

I send off the messenger at 11 with my answer in the affirmative.[2]

*Cliveden. March 16. Midnight.*

I. *Memorandum by the Queen, 12 March*[3]

12 March 1873.

Memorandum of the Queen's first interview with Mr. Gladstone.

I have just seen Mr. Gladstone. I told him I was not surprised at the result for his letters had led me to expect it. He said, to the *last* there had been *great* uncertainty amongst his followers as to the result. He thinks the defeat was mainly owing to the declaration of the Irish Roman Catholic bishops—and that all over the world there was a great attempt to impose priestly dominion which I said must be firmly resisted to which he answered 'I hope so'. He was not prepared to say what course it would be best for the government to pursue. There were several open to them, resignation; dissolution; or to finish the session with a view to dissolution, dropping everything but what was absolutely necessary. Last year he was decidedly averse to dissolution feeling that the government would certainly lose much. This year there might be rather a more favourable chance, but there was no material change. This *question* in itself was one *on* which it would be impossible to go to the country. There were several points which he wished to name—amongst which was the one—that Mr. Bentinck, a Conservative, of some influence had stated that Mr. Hardy had declared he would *not* take office in *this* present Parliament, but though he repeated this twice before Mr. Hardy in the House the latter took no notice of it—so that it was evident he had heard this from some *private* source—for certainly it was impossible for any one to say this when his whole party joined in voting against the government. The position was an unparalleled one, from this circumstance viz. the change that had suddenly taken place in the feeling *on* the Bill. From all sides he had heard when it was first proposed expressions of its being fair and just and likely to pass and now within the last fortnight every one was against it! The Bill was *not* absolutely lost for from the mode of voting any one might still propose

[1] Guedalla, i. no. 527.
[2] Guedalla, i. no. 528.
[3] The Royal Archives, C48/6. In the Queen's hand.

its being read a second time, though he did not think that course possible for the government to adopt. He thought the Cabinet should not come to a decision today, but tomorrow when they would meet again. He would come and see me at six today and again at a quarter to three tomorrow. He was not at all depressed.

II. *WEG's notes of the Cabinet meeting of 12 March*[1]

Cabinet. March 12. 73. 2½ p.m.

Division of last night.

WEG recommended conversation only *today*,

Glyn called in: reported conversation with Sir G. Grey who recommended resignation and thought the other side would fail to form a government.

Courses. Ignore the vote—*no*.
       Revise the bill—*no*.
       Vote of confidence.
       Resignation.
       Dissolution           }Discussed for some time.
       (immediate or postponed).

Hartington reported Irish opinions (for dissolution if *not on* Education Bill).[2]

III. *Memorandum by the Queen, 12 March*[3]

Memorandum on second interview with Mr. Gladstone March 12, 1873 at ¼ past 6 p.m.

    Mr. Gladstone said that the Cabinet had come to no decision which he thought was far better, waiting to consider and hear what was felt and thought till tomorrow morning. The various courses were considered. One was a vote of confidence, like what had been thought of in '66—which would no doubt be carried by a large majority, would be useless in the face of last night's vote and therefore *that* course was put aside. A dissolution might be possible—but he thought would *not* be favourable to government. Carrying on the government with a view to

---

[1] ADD MS 44641, f 64.
[2] See also WEG's letter to the Queen, 12 March, Guedalla, i. no. 519. A note of opinions on a question of dissolution/resignation/no confidence, undated but possibly 12 March 1873, is among the Glynne-Gladstone MSS at Hawarden.
[3] The Royal Archives, C48/11.

ultimate dissolution—though it had been done—was humiliating and difficult. *All* felt however that the vote could *not* be *passed over*.

In case of their resigning, I said, and my calling on the opposition to form a government, they might fail and I might have to call upon him to retain office—which had happened in '39 and '51—and in '45 which he said was the most *parallel case* when Sir R. Peel resigned in the autumn and Lord Russell failing to form a government, Sir R. Peel consented to carry it on which he did and carried the Corn Law Bill. But Mr. Gladstone *doubted* this happening. Mr. Bright had come to see him and urged the government remaining in—and *ignoring* the vote and dropping the Bill—as the most patriotic course; but Mr. Gladstone felt that this would never do and would lower the position of the government and only expose them to more defeats, in which I entirely concurred considering the very high tone he held about the measure in introducing it. Sir G. Grey on the other hand was for their resigning and *against* dissolution.

The country was perfectly quiet. At twelve tomorrow there was to be another Cabinet and he was to come to me at a quarter to three. He seemed very tired and worn.

IV. *WEG's notes of the Cabinet meeting of 13 March*[1]
Thursday March 13. 73.
The situation.
WEG stated the case between the two alternatives of dissolution and resignation (assuming that no other alternatives could be entertained) so far as regarded himself.
On the side of resignation it would not be necessary to make any final announcement.
I am strongly advised a temporary rest.
On the other hand if we now dissolve, I anticipate that *afterwards* before any long time difficulties will arise and our mission will terminate.
So that the alternatives are not so unequally weighted.
Information reported.
Cabinet, without any marked difference, or at least any positive assertion to the contrary, determined on tendering their resignations.
What is WEG to say to the Queen if Queen desires time.
To ask the House for it—Friday.

---

[1] ADD MS 44641, ff 74–75.

If she asks advice.

To observe the natural course is to send to the person who led the assault against the government and who was the last Prime Minister.

Tell the House.

Either has received the tender and is considering, or

Has accepted—and we hold office provisionally until other arrangements are made.

V. *Memorandum by the Queen, 13 March*[1]

Memorandum of third interview of the Queen with Mr. Gladstone, 13 March 1873.

Mr. Gladstone came at ten minutes to three. He said he had to report what the proceedings of the Cabinet had been and that he would not require to detain me long. After having had a day to consider they all were unanimous in agreeing that this was a vote which was too grave and serious to be passed over and that therefore a vote of confidence was out of the question. That they had in consequence considered the question of dissolution or resignation, and that they had come to the conclusion that the safest and best course was, with every expression of respect and gratitude to tender their resignations to me. And unless I wished for more time to consider, they would announce this to both Houses this evening. I asked if it would be better to delay or not? He answered, unless *I* wished it, it was 'most undesirable' that there should be any suspense or delay. To this I agreed, and gave him likewise permission if it was according to precedent to say in the House that I had sent for Mr. Disraeli, which it was my intention to do. He was to do so, or not according to precedent. I said it was possible that Mr. Disraeli might be unable to form a government when I would have to call upon him again. He replied, that might be but it was impossible to foresee what course the members of the government might be disposed to take then. As for himself he wished to retire altogether for a time, which I said I thought he would not be *allowed* to do. That I feared he must be very tired and he repeated that he longed for rest, for the work and exertion for body and mind were beyond what human nature could bear, and he feared the tendency was to increase instead of lessening this. He spoke of some honours which he was anxious should be bestowed on some people of distinction of which he handed me a list

---

[1] The Royal Archives, C48/16. In the Queen's hand.

and then I said: 'And what could I offer *you* in acknowledgment for your services? What would you wish?' He said nothing; he wished for nothing. He was very grateful for many blessings and for the gracious kindness he had experienced from me. When he alluded to his retiring from public life altogether for a time he said, that he did not by that mean to say that he would *not* be ready, in case there were emergencies which called for him, to give every assistance to the best of his ability. I replied I was sure I could rely on this.

I promised to let him hear as soon as I had anything to tell him.

### VI. *Memorandum by WEG, 13 March*[1]

This afternoon at half past three I left the Palace having placed at the feet of the Sovereign the ministerial resignations, which were graciously accepted. The Queen informed me that she would send for Mr. Disraeli: suggested for consideration whether I would include the mention of this fact in my announcement to Parliament: and added as I was leaving the room, without looking (apparently) for an answer, that she would inform me of what might take place.

At a quarter to seven, or a little later, Colonel Ponsonby called with a communication from Her Majesty. Any news? I said. 'A great deal', he replied: and informed me as follows. Mr. Disraeli had been with the Queen: did not see the means of carrying on the government by the agency of his party under present circumstances; did not ask for the dissolution of the Parliament (this was understood to mean did not offer to become Minister on condition of being permitted to dissolve); did not say that his renunciation of the task was final: recommended that the Queen should call for my advice. Upon this the Queen sent Colonel Ponsonby, and 'She considers this as sending for you anew.'

I replied:

That I did not regard the Queen's reference of this intelligence to me as her calling upon me anew to undertake the work of government: that none of my obligations to the Sovereign were cancelled or impaired

---

[1] ADD MS 44761, ff 102–108. Marked by WEG: 'No. 1'. The first of a collection of papers dealing with these events, mostly the correspondence of WEG and Disraeli with the Queen. Nos. 2–9, 11 and 12 are in the royal correspondence in the Gladstone Papers. No. 10 is a draft for WEG's statement to the Commons on 17 March (ADD MS 44761, ff 109–110). No. 13 is notes for a further statement on 20 March (ibid., f 112). The cover for these papers is f 92. It is docketed by WEG: 'March 1873. Papers relating to the crisis. 1–9 were circulated in the Cabinet, March 18, 19. 73.'

by the resignation tendered and accepted: that I was still the minister for the purpose of rendering any service she might be pleased to call for in the matter on which she is engaged, exactly as before, until she has a new minister, when my official obligations will come to an end.

That I felt there was great inconvenience, and danger of misapprehension out of doors, in proceeding over rapidly with a matter of such gravity, and that each step in it required to be well measured and ascertained before proceeding to consider of the next following step.

That I had great difficulty in gathering any precise idea of Mr. Disraeli's account of what he could not do, and what he either could or did not say that he could not. That as this account was to present to me the state of facts on which I was commanded to advise, it was quite necessary for me to have an accurate idea of it, in order that I might do justice to Her Majesty's commands. I would therefore humbly suggest that Mr. Disraeli might with great propriety be requested to put his reply into writing. That I presumed I might receive this reply if it were Her Majesty's pleasure to make it known to me at some not late hour tomorrow, when I would at once place myself in a condition to tender my humble advice.

This is an account of what Colonel Ponsonby might fairly consider as my answer to Her Majesty's communication. I enlarged the conversation however by observing that the division which overthrew us was a party division: it bore the express authentic symbol of its character in having party tellers on the opposition as well as the government side: that we were aware of the great, even more than ordinary efforts of Colonel Taylor, with Mr. Disraeli's countenance, to bring Members to London (the £85 story) and to the House; that all this seemed to impose great obligations on the opposition; and if so that it would be the duty of the leader of opposition to use every exertion of consultation with his friends and otherwise before declining the task or in any manner advising the Queen to look elsewhere. To Colonel Ponsonby indeed I observed that I thought Mr. Disraeli was endeavouring by at once throwing back on me an offer which it was impossible for me at the time and under the circumstances to accept, to get up a case of absolute necessity founded upon this refusal of mine and thus becoming the indispensable man and party to have in his hands a lever wherewith to overcome the reluctance and resistance of his friends who would not be able to deny that the Queen must have a government.

*March 13. 1873.*

VII. *Memorandum by the Queen, 15 March*[1]
Memorandum of the Queen's fourth interview with Mr. Gladstone, 15 March 1873.

I saw Mr. Gladstone at three and told him that I had received his long letter and asked whether he wished me to forward it to Mr. Disraeli? He left that to me; I then asked what did *he* exactly *wish* me to ask Mr. Disraeli and he replied in the sense of the last sentence of his letter, which he wished should be conveyed to Mr. Disraeli though I told him he had told me he was entirely agreed with his former colleagues. Mr. Gladstone said he had not got that in writing and that it was impossible that they (many of whom were absent) should be *aware before* the *fact* of what *took place after it.* That it was most important that the country should know there was no shuffling of cards—and that they should not think this was a preconceived plan of mock resignation in order to resume power; and that until it was absolutely *clear* that Mr. Disraeli had consulted his party and would not form a government he did not like to call on his colleagues to consider whether they could go on. It would be a very serious question, for this vote was a severe blow and that they would not be in the same position they were in before. I repeated to him what Mr. Disraeli had said about the vote, and also that in case no one else could go on with the government he would be ready to do so. I thought it best *not* to ask what Mr. Gladstone would do in case Mr. Disraeli again declined, but to wait till I heard from him.

**281** 17 February 1874 *Audience with the Queen: the resignation of Ministers*
ADD MS 44762 f 28

*The Liberals were defeated at the general election of 1874, and the Cabinet decided to resign without meeting Parliament.*

I was with the Queen today at Windsor for three quarters of an hour, and nothing could be more frank, natural, and kind, than her manner throughout.

In conversation at the audience, I of course followed the line on which we agreed last night.[2] She assented freely to all the honours I had

---

[1] The Royal Archives, C48/38. In the Queen's hand.
[2] To resign if recommendations to honours were accepted. ADD MS 44641, f 259.

proposed. There was therefore no impediment whatever to the immediate and plenary execution of my commission from the Cabinet: and I at once tendered our resignations, which I understand to have been graciously accepted.

She left me, I have no doubt, to set about making other arrangements.

We shall be duly informed of the day of final farewell.[1]

*11 Carlton House Terrace. February 17. 1874.*

**282** 25 May 1878 *Conversation with Lord Carnarvon: the Queen's relations with the Cabinet*
ADD MS 44763 ff 130–131

*Secret.*
Yesterday I saw Carnarvon, whose conversation was remarkable.[2] He said significantly he had lost most of his faith in the words of many men. We had been talking of his (old) colleagues—and he pointed to Cross. But what I wish particularly to record are two statements given in the strictest confidence, which show how little at present within the royal precinct liberty is safe.

1. It has happened repeatedly not only that Cabinet ministers have been sent for to receive 'wiggings' from the Queen—which as he said it is their affair and fault if they allow to impair their independence—but communications have from time to time been made to the Cabinet warning it off from certain subjects and saying she could not agree to this and could not agree to that.

2. The Prince of Wales has said to Carrington, who is his friend, that when he comes to the Throne he intends to be his own Foreign Minister. (Why not learn the business first?)

On the first of these I said it recalled James II and the Bill of Rights to which he assented. It is at any rate a position much more advanced than that of George III who I apprehend limited himself to a case of conscience like the Coronation Oath. But that controversy was decided

---

[1] For the Queen's account of this audience, see her memorandum, *L.Q.V.*, 2nd series, ii. 317–319. Granville told the Queen that WEG returned from Windsor 'quite "under the charm" '. Ibid., 319.

[2] Carnarvon had resigned from the Cabinet on 24 January.

once for all when George IV after a terrible struggle agreed to the Roman Catholic Emancipation Bill.

I said that such an outrage as this was wholly new, totally unknown in every Cabinet in which I had served; and that the corruption must be regarded as due to Lord Beaconsfield, which he entirely felt.

As to the second point I said that if it were realised the Prince made King would not only be his own Foreign Minister, but would probably find that he would have his Foreign Office in foreign parts.

*May 26. 1878.*

**283** 24 November–8 December 1879  *WEG's itinerary of his first Midlothian campaign, with an estimate of the size of his audiences*
ADD MS 44763 ff 164–165

1879.

| | | |
|---|---|---:|
| Mon. Nov. 24 | 1. Carlisle | 500 |
| | 2. Hawick | 4,000 |
| | 3. Galashiels | 8,000 |
| Tues. 25 | 4. Edinburgh Music Hall | 2,500 |
| | 5. Edinburgh City Hall | 250 |
| Wed. 26 | 6. Dalkeith Corn Exchange | 3,500 |
| | 7. Dalkeith Ladies and Committee | 750 |
| Thursd. 27 | 8. West Calder Assembly | 3,500 |
| | 9. Dalmeny, after dinner | 50 |
| Friday 28 | 10. Dalmeny, Leith address | 50 |
| Sat. 29 | 11. Edinburgh Corn Exchange | 5,000 |
| | 12. Edinburgh Waverley Market | 20,000 |
| Mon. Dec. 1 | 13. Inverkeithing address | 500 |
| | 14. Dunfermline ditto | 3,000 |
| | 15. Perth, freedom | 1,500 |
| | 16. Perth, open air addresses | 4,000 |
| | 17. Aberfeldie, address | 500 |
| Tues. Dec. 2 | 18. Killin address, Taymouth | 50 |
| Thurs. Dec. 4 | 19. Sir J. Watson's, after dinner | 30 |
| Fri. Dec. 5 | 20. Inaugural address Glasgow | 5,000 |
| | 21. University luncheon | 150 |
| | 22. St. Andrew's Hall | 6,500 |
| | | 69,330[1] |

---

[1] End of f 164.

| Fri. Dec. 5 | 23. City Hall | 2,500 |
| Sat. Dec. 6 | 24. Motherwell, addresses | 2,000 |
| | 25. Hamilton freedom (Dalziel) | 100 |
| Mon. Dec. 8 | 26. Carlisle, station | 1,000 |
| | 27. Preston, station | 2,000 |
| | 28. Wigan, outside ditto | 6,000 |
| | 29. Warrington, station | 1,000 |
| | 30. Chester, procession | 3,000 |
| | | 17,600 |
| | Brought over | 69,330 |
| | | 86,930 |

There were speeches running from six to eight minutes up to an hour and three quarters. There were some shorter addresses to crowds at stations, and acknowledgments of votes of thanks.

Those above given occupied about 15½ hours.     *December 11. 1879.*

**284** 8 February 1880 '*Memorandum on the religious profession of my sister Helen Jane Gladstone*'[1]
ADD MS 44764 ff 1–10

Memorandum on the religious profession of my sister Helen Jane Gladstone.

Born June 28. 1814
Died January 16. 1880

WEG February 8. 1880.
Perused and a few words inserted, September 21. 1880.

I propose to put down, before the traces of them in my mind become feebler than they now are, various particulars of evidence bearing upon the religious profession of my dear sister Helen Jane Gladstone, during her later years and on her deathbed. The call for such a record lies in the following conjunction of circumstances. It was I think in the summer of 1842 that she announced to her family her having entered the communion of the Roman Church. But on the 27th of January 1880

[1] For WEG's sister Helen Jane, see S. G. Checkland, *The Gladstones: a Family Biography, 1764–1851,* 1971.

she was buried at Fasque, Kincardineshire, with the Anglican rite, in the family vault underneath the episcopal chapel of that place: the persons directly responsible for this arrangement being my brother Sir Thomas Gladstone and myself. Let me begin by stating that, for my share in the matter, I have felt myself under the most sacred obligation to proceed judicially, and to exclude from my mind, to the best of my ability, everything in the nature of sectarian or ecclesiastical pre-possession. I have done what I think an upright Roman Catholic brother would have been bound to do; namely, in the absence of a direct statement of her wishes, to examine the evidence bearing upon the point, and to act upon it if sufficient. When I had gone through this process at Cologne, I opened my mind to my brother as follows: it is my conviction, I said, that in loyalty to her we are absolutely bound, when we take her remains to England, to exclude any inter-position of a Roman priest properly so called in the funeral obsequies. He had arrived at the same conclusion. I added that there would in my opinion be a different case for consideration, if there were any church of those termed Old Catholics in England or Scotland: but, there being no such church, the case does not arise. She was herself, as I knew, aware of the fact that no such organisation existed for she had, some years before, desired me to inquire about it from Bishop Reinkens.

Besides my sense of the high duty of loyalty to her, I regard the change in her religious position as a matter of importance, and of interest to others, in this respect; that, although I am far from saying hers was the most powerful mind of all the persons who in our country have seceded to the Church of Rome within the last forty years, yet I think it was the most powerful among all the women (so far as I know) who have taken that step, and the most powerful among those whether men or women, who, having taken the step, have reverted or shown a disposition to revert to the communion of the Church of England. Among these I include the excellent Mr. R. Waldo Sibthorp who was by his own direction buried in the Anglican Church.

I divide the evidence according as it was derived

1. From Mrs. Watkins her attached and faithful maid through thirty-two years;
2. From circumstantial indications;
3. From Mr. Henkel;
4. From my own direct intercourse during the last ten years.

I. The maid Mrs. Watkins is a steady, quiet, and religious Roman

Catholic of the old school, much opposed to Vaticanism, but not having in consequence of it ceased to receive the ordinances of the Church from those likeminded with herself.

During the last illness she stated to me that two priests, I think from the cathedral, had been to Disch's Hotel to press upon her (one or both) for admission to Mrs. Helen's bedside, urging the motives of edification or of scandal. They seemed to have pressed her hard, and she consulted me. I said (this was before we had ceased to hope) what does the doctor say? She replied, 'The doctor (Schmidts) is against it; and Mrs. Helen is against it.' I said, 'If the doctor is against it, you cannot be entitled to take the matter out of his hands: tell them to go [to] the doctor and lay the case before him instead of trying to work upon you.'

One of these priests came to the hotel I think on the morning after our arrival (Tuesday), but was not admitted to the apartment. I heard of no further effort.

On the morning of Thursday the 15th of January Mrs. Watkins came to me and said a priest was with her, who came from the country, and was an Old Catholic, but who would not be recognised as an Old Catholic among the clergy of Cologne. Making inquiry I found his name was Focher, he had a parish in the country I think near Darnagen: he had seen her (not I imagine for any rite) some months before: he had not now been sent for but came of his own accord. Very shortly after, he came out, and desired to see me. He told me he found her very ill, had but few words with her, and offered a short prayer. He did not say whether at her request. He described to me his position in the diocese from which I gathered distinctly that he was under the archbishop who I understood had promised to promote him but did not: he was recommended by Dr. Schmidts and reputed I apprehend to stand well with the liberal Roman Catholics.

Mrs. Watkins shortly after came to me and said, 'I told Mrs. Helen he had asked to see you and was with you. She said I am glad of that for he (my brother) will be able to tell me whether he is a good one.' This puzzled me a little at the time: but afterwards I construed it to mean whether he was one of those under the jurisdiction of Bishop Reinkens. I think Mrs. Watkins added he would say a mass for her the next day, and she felt sure Mrs. Helen would be glad of this.

On the evening of the death Mrs. Watkins said to me 'Tomorrow I shall get a mass said for her, as Mrs. Helen would have liked that.' I said 'Please let it be on your account and not in any manner as from my brother or me.' This was to be by the priest as I understood to whom Mrs. Watkins resorted, as one of the older school.

We asked Mrs. Watkins whether she was aware what our sister's wishes had been as to burial. She replied 'Oh she always wished to be buried at Fasque—I never had a doubt of her wishing to be buried at Fasque.' In corroboration of this, as she thought, she produced something my sister had said to her to the effect 'that they would return to England and that she would visit Fasque once again, and Mrs. Watkins with her'. This she construed as I have said with reference to burial.

She also said to me 'Mrs. Helen died a Catholic, perhaps an Old Catholic.' This is all I think that came from her with direct reference to the subject of religious profession: but she mentioned other matters as to her having given over her property (in the years immediately following my father's death), as to her subsequent regret, and as to the change (somewhere about 1862) in her relations with Cardinal Wiseman.

II. The circumstantial evidence is various. Among its leading particulars must certainly stand, with the repulsion of the priests of the cathedral, the fact that she had not for many years, I apprehend since the Vatican Council, received any of the rites of the Roman Church. There is every sign that the time has passed in the unintermitted exercise of private devotion. I find the draft of a letter written in June 1875, but apparently not sent, which shows that the question was then before her mind whether she could ask absolution from a priest in communion with Rome 'without making a previous statement of (what I must own to be forbid) strong convictions respecting all that is now held to be essentially Roman doctrine'. This letter proves in the negative form the date of those 'strong convictions'. (The explanation seems to be that as we know abundantly she lived in the never abandoned intention of coming to England, but that she felt her return would of necessity bring about some decisive step in regard to religious profession, and that she allowed herself for that and other reasons to continue indefinitely and almost from week to week this postponement.)

After her death, I passed through my hands all that part of her collection of books at Cologne, which had not been packed for London, about 2,000 volumes I think, with periodicals and newspapers to boot: and I made a careful examination of her books of devotion. As to newspapers she did not take in one which represented Roman Catholic interests: but she took in the (London) *Guardian*. As to periodicals, of

which she took large numbers, I found among them *The Month* but Mrs. Watkins told me my sister had promised it to her: and not in any one of the numbers which I saw was there a single leaf cut open. She had a very large supply of novels and tales. Not one of them was Roman Catholic, or, so far as I know, by a Roman Catholic writer; but there were many scores of the tales published by the (Anglican) Society for Promoting Christian Knowledge. Lastly, as to her books of devotion. Many of the distinctly Roman Catholic books of this class bear the marks of long use. But of these not one is dated after 1870. There are on the other hand two or three such books dated I think between 1870 and 1873: but of these not any bear the marks of having been used. There was a small volume in her library of the Prayers of Saint Anselm with an introduction by Cardinal Manning: this looked new as from the shop. On the other hand there was a portable English psalter, from the Prayer Book, greatly worn and dog-eared. The type of this had been too small, of late, for her eyes affected with incipient cataract; and she had provided herself with a New Testament and Psalter of the S.P.C.K. in large type. This, said Mrs. Watkins, always lay on her bed and was used by her daily. There was also a large type edition of *The Christian Year*, much used; of which Mrs. Watkins told me that this likewise lay on her bed for constant use and that if by any accident it were mislaid for half a day she could not bear it. There were other books of large type, the set called Lyra with different epithets, which Mrs. Watkins said she loved and used. Mrs. Watkins's impression was that she had not disused some old Roman Catholic books which were in a tray near her bed. There were no emblems of religion, not even I think a Cross, visible in the room; but she wore a crucifix under her clothes. This evidence, taken in the aggregate, appears to me very important in the case of one who had not passed under any religious chill, though it would have been of little force had there been room for the supposition that it merely formed a part of a wider negative process.
III. Mr. Henkel is a Protestant German with whom she had become acquainted at Cologne, perhaps in transactions at the bank for her purposes of business: and I at once gathered that she esteemed him, because, soon after my arrival, she expressed her great desire that I should see him. On the morning after the decease (the 17th) he came to us and expressed a desire to be of service to us at the Rathaus in connection with the formalities required by law. I do not remember whether he had then already done something but we were glad to make

use of his friendly aid and he went backwards and forwards for the purpose. He told us that the religious profession required to be registered and that he proposed to give in 'Old Catholic'. I asked him upon what authority, and he replied that she had expressly and repeatedly stated to him as a fact that she was *Alt-Katholik*. This being so, we agreed with him and asked him to give it on his own credit as a witness, not in our names. Afterwards he returned and announced that the law would allow of *Anglicanisch* or *Griechisch*, but not of any distinction subaltern to those of *Katholik* and *Evangelisch*. All the Old Catholics of Cologne were registered on death by the simple name *Katholik*. We had no authority to call her *Anglicanisch*, and under the circumstances thus ascertained, we agreed to the legal designation, taking care however to put the facts on paper in letters between Herr Henkel and myself.

IV. Under the head of evidence drawn from my own direct intercourse with my sister, I must first observe that I write from memory without preliminary reference to documents; and also that I do not aim at giving every word of what she spoke to me on her deathbed.

For many years she had been, so to speak, opening out to me on the subject of religion and religious profession. For the present purpose it is enough to refer to what took place in 1874, when I spent some days at Cologne on my way back from Munich, in the hope of effectually stirring her to return to England. I found that she was in complete sympathy with Dr. Döllinger then recently excommunicated, who at her request came over (unless I mistake) from Bonn to see her. I had been in very full communication with him at Munich which I reported without reserve to her, as to a person entirely feeling with him. At her express desire I wrote a letter, though personally a stranger, to Bishop Reinkens, to inquire from him whether there was any congregation or body in England with whom he was in communion. (The reply was in the negative.) She inquired of me about the episcopal succession in the Church of England, and apprised me that her doubts on the subject of this succession had had a large I think she said the main share in bringing her within the Roman fold. She seemed well pleased with what I told her on this subject: and somewhat later she wrote to me and asked for a statement of the case; which I sent her. She spoke of the difficulty in which going to England would place her as it would require some step.

We reached Cologne on Monday, January 12 at noon. On that day and the following one we were growingly hopeful as to her recovery:

and there was no reference to religion in such conversation as I had with her except it were in very general terms, the objects being her repose and health. On Wednesday (probably) it was that in speaking to me she recited earnestly the words *In manus tuas Domine commendo spiritum meum.* I asked her 'Shall I say the Lord's Prayer?' She eagerly accepted, and I knelt down and repeated it slowly in Latin, she responding to every clause. I then recited verse 6 of Psalm 51. *Asperges me hyssopo et mundabor; lavabis me et super nivem dealbabor.*[1] All these words she recited after me with still greater fervour. I then or later in the day repeated in English the verses of Psalm 121. 'I will lift up mine eyes unto the hills' and she took them with the same animated devotion, and showed no less familiarity with the language. Again on the Thursday (I think) I said the Paternoster. I think it was on the Friday that I began the verses 'Come unto me', and she said yes, yes, but that she was too weak. Her mind was entirely clear on all these occasions but she was not in strength enough for sustained, only for fragmentary, attention and exertion.

On these days, beginning with Wednesday, I said to her repeatedly, 'Helen, have you anything to say? Have you any wishes? You know how sacred they will be with us.' She answered on each occasion that she had, but that she was not strong enough. Once she said 'If I speak it will kill me.' Once in answer to my inquiry, she said a few emphatic words about her maid's money-matters, 'Whatever Watkins tells you about her money, do it.' It was after this that, when I asked her whether she had anything more to say she made the reply I have last quoted. When I told Mrs. Watkins my sister had expressed a great desire to say something to me, she at once said 'That will be something relating to religion.' Late on Thursday indeed she said once she had nothing more to ask: but this was just after some little matter had been arranged about her bed. The secret never was revealed. But she continued to speak in terms of fond affection. On the Thursday looking fixedly at me she said 'I think we shall meet again' and after a moment or two 'I hope we shall meet again'. On that day the use of the Lord's Prayer at once recalled and subdued her from a state of excited *malaise* in a most remarkable manner. That afternoon she wandered a little under the influence of what the doctors had then for the first time given her.

---

[1] This is verse 7 of Psalm 51 (Psalm 50 in the Vulgate). WEG wrote 'supra' for 'super'.

She said 'Why did he come to tease me, talking about the mote and the beam?' This was said twice: and Mrs. Watkins told her no one had been speaking about the mote and the beam. 'Did not they?' she said, 'then it was only my wicked heart; my wicked heart.' I must add yet one incident. On the Wednesday I said 'I am delighted to hear that your chief physician (the Professor) is among the very first in Germany.' She replied 'And they made an Ultramontane trouble about him here, about his coming to the hospital.' And went on, 'And so they have been making now an Ultramontane trouble about me': referring no doubt to the efforts at entry which I have mentioned. But she told me with great pleasure that she knew many were praying for her in the churches.

On Thursday we had no solid hope remaining. Friday was a day of waiting for death, who much quickened his pace as he came near. Almost or quite her last words were for the care of her birds, after her. Sore had been some of the chastisements of the illness: but the last three hours were peace: in a wonderful manner, youth and beauty came back upon her worn face for the moment, and she looked half her age. With death returned the looks of death. 'God accept her, Christ receive her.'                                          *February 8. 1880.*

*WEG to Lord Acton, 26 January 1880*[1]

... Your first emotion may perhaps be one of surprise or misgiving when I tell you she will be buried here [Fasque] tomorrow with the Anglican rite. She will lie in the family vault under the episcopal chapel by the side of her father and mother. Of that vault my brother is master. Of her desire to rest in it we are assured by her maid, an excellent woman of the pre-Vatican Roman Catholic fashion. But I entirely agree with the proceeding. The evidence is abundant which shows that it would have been treason to her memory and wishes to allow of her being buried by a priest of the actual Roman Church. I have had no opportunity of giving this evidence fully to anyone, except Sir R. Phillimore, in whose judicial habit of mind I have confidence, and who after patiently hearing it said there could be no doubt. There would have been another aspect of the case had there been an Old Catholic organisation in this country, for to one witness at least in Cologne within my knowledge she declared herself repeatedly to be *Alt Katholik*. On the day after the death I wrote to Dr. Döllinger, telling him all I then could, and very desirous of any counsel he could give, but no

---

[1] ADD MS 44093, ff 209–214. Copy from the Acton papers.

answer reached Cologne before we left it on the 21st, nor have I yet any. . . .

In closing this imperfect and (for the post hour impending) hasty account let me again assure you how anxious I am—if you accept the confidence—to speak to you on the subject fully and without reserve.

*WEG to Lord Acton, 6 March 1880*[1]
I send you a short notice of the last few days of my sister; and I now wish to ask you a question concerning her.

I found among her papers (which were all scattered, and as yet have been but imperfectly examined) the draft or *abbozzo* of a letter to you which, as it is at Hawarden, I can now only roughly describe.

It requested you to learn from Dr. Döllinger whether in his judgment she, *rejecting as she did all the doctrine now proclaimed to be needful in the Roman Church*, could properly go to confession with a view to the Holy Sacrament without mentioning that rejection.

I think the words I have underlined, and which are nearly her words, mean the doctrine made in 1870.

What I beg you to tell me is whether you ever received this letter? Probably not. The draft does not look to me as if she had sent it. It was dated I think in 1874.

I am given to understand that in Roman circles here [London] I am accused (it should be my brother and I) of disregarding her wishes in not having her buried with the rites of the Anglo-Roman Church.

Such disregard I should consider to be not only an error but a crime. I do not think there was in her later years any Roman Catholic with whom she lived in intimacy: or I would not scruple to submit to such a person the whole evidence in the case as far as I have been able to put it together. I have never authorised any statement that she died 'a Protestant'. My *impression* is that there was no great change in her belief except as to Vaticanism. My *convictions* are that she died in fervent faith and in true penitence, *and* not in the actual Roman communion. For this is, I presume, wholly excluded by her describing herself as 'Alt Katholik'. Of course I claim no infallibility of judgment in this matter; but I think myself impartial, because of the horror (it is not less) with which I regard any tampering or trafficking in these most solemn subjects. . . .

---

[1] Ibid., ff 215–217. Copy from the Acton papers. Marked 'Most private'.

*Lord Acton to WEG, 11 March 1880*[1]
Your enquiry dated March 6, reached me only yesterday.

I never received the letter in question, nor any other letter from Miss Gladstone. But some conversation passed between us which bore upon the same subject.

In June 1875 Lady Acton stayed for some days at the Hotel Disch, where we were well known, as we came often, with a family of children, occupying the same rooms, and giving a good deal of trouble. The housemaid talked to her about the guest who had been so long in the house and no doubt Miss Gladstone learnt from her that I was expected. She sent for me, and without, I think, putting the exact question you mention, described her own position and enquired earnestly about that of men like Strossmayer and Kenrick who disbelieved the Vatican decrees, and remained in the Roman communion. I carried away the impression that it had been agreable to her to talk these matters over, but nothing showed that my explanations had satisfied her in regard to what was personal to herself.

She spoke of herself as disbelieving the Vatican system as defined in 1870, but it seemed that she would willingly have heard that there was some interpretation which would justify her in remaining where she was. Neither the alternative of Anglicanism, nor that of suspended churchmanship, if I may use the term, appeared to be before her. And I do not remember that the proximity of the Bonn divines was adverted to. For I must repeat that she was not asking for advice, but for information, although her purpose in asking for it was not at all disguised.

We were told, by the informant I have mentioned, that the parish priest had given her communion in her sick room. I cannot remember whether we heard this on the occasion of our visit in 1875, or on a later journey in 1878. I should be inclined to think the latter date more probable, but Lady Acton cannot call to mind any conversation of the kind on that occasion. This is a question of fact which Miss Gladstone's maid could settle.

Assuming my information to be false, the question arises: would she have preferred to receive absolution and communion from a priest of the Church of Rome who knew her state of mind, or from the Bonn divines? I believe she would have preferred the former. If not, if she held herself to be separated from Rome, it seems likely that she would

---

[1] Ibid., ff 219–220.

have asked to see Reusch or Langen. If she did not ask for them, it would appear that she was only restrained from sending for the parish priest by the fear of his raising objections. Her declaration that she was Alt Katholik does not appear to me to prove that she was not in the actual Roman communion. For the term may designate a person who rejects that communion, or who is rejected by it, who excludes himself, or who is excluded by others. I do not understand that she belonged to the first of these categories.

There is of course much essential evidence of which I know nothing, and I do not presume to suggest an opinion beyond the question you put to me.

What remains for me to add will, I fear, damage my testimony. Lady Acton has a very vague impression that Miss Gladstone did write to me. It might be that she wrote to desire that I would consult Döllinger, and that, not having had to answer the question, but only to convey it, the letter afterwards slipped from my memory. But it may also be that Lady Acton confounds conversation and correspondence. I cannot speak so positively as I did in beginning my letter.

The uncertainty of my recollection will excuse me, I hope, in your eyes, for having taken Lady Acton into my confidence regarding what passed formerly, though not as to the contents of your letter. . . .

*WEG to Lord Acton, 14 March 1880*[1]
I thank you very much for your letter. The question about my sister is one of deep interest, and I shall continue to gather every fragment of information about it although no practical judgment remains to be formed. The only point on which I am inclined to differ from what seems to be your opinion is as to the use of the word Alt Katholik under the circumstances of the case. If Bishop Strossmayer were to use that word the sense of it would be qualified by the fact that he remained in the exercise of his office, and it would mean an opinion not a profession. But in my sister's case all the evidence is the other way. I will learn at some proper time, or rather re-learn, from Mrs. Watkins, her maid, what is the fact as to the housemaid's story. In the mean time I am pretty sure that there was nothing of the kind in 1878 or for years before. In 1874 I saw her and had much conversation with her. She was then seriously thinking of re-joining the Church of England, but I have

[1] Ibid., ff 223–225. Copy from the Acton papers.

47

a moral certainty that what would have pleased her best would have been to find that an Old Catholic communion had taken root in England. She made me write for her to Bishop Reinkens to learn whether there was anything of the kind. Probably I told you in my letter that in her last illness she would not see the priests (from the cathedral, as Mrs. Watkins described them) who tried hard to get in by very improperly influencing the maid, but in vain. All this being in fragments is simply confusing you. *All* that I know is at your service if you like to see it when in England. In the meantime I certainly have not a doubt that her friend Herr Henckel was right in describing her after death to the authorities as Alt Katholik; although that does not without taking other facts into view determine the propriety of the course taken by my brother and me in England.

**285**  22 April 1880  *Conversation with Lord Hartington: Hartington's audience with the Queen*
ADD MS 44764 ff 43–47

*Parliament was dissolved on 24 March 1880. The general election resulted in a Liberal majority, and on 21 April Beaconsfield resigned. The next day the Queen sent for Hartington.*

*Secret.*
April 22. 1880 at seven p.m. Hartington came to see me at Wolverton's house and reported on his journey to Windsor.

The Queen stood with her back to the window—which *used* not to be her custom. On the whole I gathered that her manner was more or less embarrassed but towards him not otherwise than gracious and confiding.

She told him that she desired him to form an administration and pressed upon him strongly his duty to assist her as a responsible leader of the party now in a large majority. I could not find that she expressed clearly her reason for appealing to him as a responsible leader of the party, and yet going past *the* leader of the party, namely Granville, whom no one except himself has a title to displace. She, however, indicated to him her confidence in his moderation, the phrase under which he is daily commended in the *Daily Telegraph*, at this moment I think Beaconsfield's personal organ, and the recipient of his inspirations. By his moderation the Queen intimated that Hartington was distinguished from Granville as well as from me.

Hartington in reply to Her Majesty made becoming acknowledgments and proceeded to say that he did not think a government could be satisfactorily formed without me: he had not had any direct communication with me: but he had reason to believe that I would not take any office or post in the government except that of First Minister. Under these circumstances he advised Her Majesty to place the matter in my hands. The Queen continued to urge upon him the obligations arising out of his position and desired him to ascertain whether he was right in his belief that I would not act in a ministry unless as First Minister. This he said is a question which I should not have put to you except when desired by the Queen.

I said Her Majesty was quite justified I thought in requiring positive information and he therefore in putting the question to me. Of my action he was already in substantial possession as it had been read to him (he had told me) by Wolverton. I am not asked I said for reasons but only for Aye or No and consequently I have only to say that I adhere to my reply as you have already conveyed it to the Queen.

In making such a reply, it was my duty to add that in case a government should be formed by him, or by Granville with him, whom the Queen seemed to me wrongly to have passed by—it was to Granville that I had resigned my trust, and he Hartington was subsequently elected by the party to the leadership in the House of Commons—my duty would be plain. It would be to give them all the support in my power, both negatively, as by absence or non-interference, and positively. Promises of this kind I said stood on slippery ground and must always be understood with the limits which might be prescribed by conviction. I referred to the extreme caution, almost costiveness, of Peel's replies to Lord Russell when he was endeavouring to form a government in December 1845 for the purpose of carrying the repeal of the Corn Law. In this case however I felt a tolerable degree of confidence because I was not aware of any substantive divergence of ideas between us, and I had observed with great satisfaction, when his address to N.E. Lancashire came into my hands after the writing but before the publication of mine to Midlothian, that they were in marked accordance as to opinions if not as to form and tone, and I did not alter a word. In the case of the first Palmerston government I had certainly been thrown into rather sharp opposition after I quitted it but this was

49

mainly due to finance—I had not approved of the finance of Sir George Lewis, highly as I estimated his judgment in general politics: and it was in some ways a relief to me, when we had become colleagues in the second Palmerston government, to find that he did not approve of mine. However I could only make such a declaration as the nature of the case allowed.

He received all this without comment, and said his conversation with Her Majesty had ended as it began each party adhering to the ground originally taken up. He had not altered his advice but had come under Her Majesty's command to learn my intentions, which he was to make known to Her Majesty returning to Windsor *this* day at one.

He asked me what I thought of the doctrine of obligation so much pressed upon him by the Queen.

I said that in my opinion the case was clear enough. Her Majesty had not always acted on the rule of sending for the leader of the opposition. Palmerston was the known and recognised leader of the opposition in 1859; but the Queen sent for Granville. The leader if sent for was in my opinion bound either to serve himself or to point out some other course to Her Majesty which he might deem to be more for the public advantage. And if that course should fail in consequence of the refusal of the person pointed out, the leader of the party could not leave Her Majesty unprovided with a government but would be bound in loyalty to undertake the task.

I did not indicate nor did he ask what I should do if sent for. He did not indicate nor did I ask what he should do if the Queen continued to press him to go on in spite of his advice to her to move in another direction.                                                           *April 23. 1880.*

**286**  23 April 1880  *Conversation with Lords Granville and Hartington: WEG summoned to Windsor*
ADD MS 44764 ff 48–49[1]

Soon after half past three today Lord Granville and Lord Hartington arrived from Windsor at my house, and signified to me the Queen's command that I should repair to Windsor where she would see me at half past six.

The purport of Lord Hartington's conversation with me yesterday

---

[1] On Windsor Castle notepaper.

had been signified. They had jointly advised hereupon that I should be sent for with a view to the formation of a government, and Her Majesty desired Lord Granville would convey to me the message. I did not understand that there had been any lengthened audience, or any reference to details.

Receiving this intimation I read to them an extract (herewith)[1] from an article in the *Daily News* of yesterday descriptive of their position relatively to me, and of mine to them, and then said that, letting drop the epithets, so I understood the matter. I presumed therefore that under the circumstances as they were established before their audience they had unitedly advised the Sovereign that it was most for the public advantage to send for me. To this they assented. I expressed, a little later, my sense of the high honour and patriotism with which they had acted: said that I had endeavoured to fulfil my own duty but was aware I might be subject to severe criticism for my resignation of the leadership five years ago, which I had forced upon them: but I did it believing in good faith that we were to have quiet times and for the first years 1875 and 1876 to the end of the session I had acted in a manner conformable to that resignation and had only been driven from my course by[2] compulsion. They made no reply but Granville had previously told me he was perfectly satisfied as to my communications with him.

I at once asked whether I might reckon, as I hoped, on their co-operation in the government.

(Resumed April 25.) Both assented. Granville agreed to take the Foreign Office, but modestly and not as of right. I proposed the Indian Office as next, or as very near, in weight, and perhaps the most difficult of all at this time, to Hartington, which he desired time to consider. I named Childers as the most proper person for the War Office. As I had to prepare for Windsor our interview was not very long: and they agreed to come again after dinner.

We spoke of the Governor Generalship—at least I spoke to Granville who staid a little after Hartington and I said Goschen's position as to the franchise would prevent his being in the Cabinet now: but he should be in great employ. Granville had had the lead in the conversation: and said the Queen requested *him* to carry the message to me.

*April 25. 1880.*

---

[1] Missing.

[2] MS reads 'my'.

**287**  23 April 1880  *Audience with the Queen: WEG commissioned to form a Ministry*
ADD MS 44764 ff 50–55[1]

Windsor
April 23. 1880.

At 6.50 I went to the Queen who received me with perfect courtesy from which she never deviates. Her Majesty presumed I was in possession of the purport of her communications with Lord Granville and with Lord Hartington; and wished to know, as the administration of Lord Beaconsfield had been 'turned out' whether I was prepared to form a government. She thought she had acted constitutionally in sending for the recognised leaders of the party and referring the matter to them in the first instance.

I said that if I might presume to speak, nothing could in my view be more correct than Her Majesty's view that the application should be so made (I did not refer to the case as *between* Lord Granville and Lord Hartington) and that it would have been an error to pass them by and refer to me.

They had stood I said between me and the position of a candidate for office, and it was only their advising Her Majesty to lay her commands upon me which could warrant my thinking of it after all that had occurred. But since they had given this advice it was not consistent with my duty to shrink from any responsibility which I had incurred, and I was aware that I had incurred a very great responsibility. I therefore humbly accepted Her Majesty's commission.

Her Majesty wished to know, in order that she might acquaint Lord Beaconsfield, whether I could undertake to form a government or whether I only meant that I would make the attempt.

I said I had obtained the cooperation of Lord Granville and Lord Hartington, and that my knowledge and belief as to prevailing dispositions would I think warrant me in undertaking to form a government; it being Her Majesty's pleasure. I had ascertained that Lord Granville would be willing to accept the Foreign Office; and I had also to say that the same considerations which made it my duty to accept office seemed also to make it my duty to submit myself to Her Majesty's pleasure for the office of Chancellor of the Exchequer together with that of First Lord of the Treasury.

---

[1] On Windsor Castle notepaper.

She asked if I had thought of any one for the War Office which was very important—the report of the commission would show that Lord Cardwell's system of short service had entirely broken down, and that a change must be made at any rate as regarded the non-commissioned officers. Lord Hartington had assured her that no one was committed to the system except Lord Cardwell and he was very unwell and hardly able to act. Lord Hartington knew the War Office and she thought would make a good War Minister.

I said that it seemed to me in the present state of the country the first object was to provide for the difficulties of statesmanship and then to deal with those of administration. The greatest of all these difficulties I thought centered in the Indian Office and I was very much inclined to think Lord Hartington would be eminently qualified to deal with them and would thereby take a place in the government suitable to his position and his probable future.

She asked to whom then did I think of entrusting the War Office?

(Resumed here April 24.) I said Mr. Childers occurred to me as an administrator of eminent capacity and conciliatory in his modes of action—his mind would be open on the grave subjects treated by the commission which did not appear to me to be even for Lord Cardwell matters of committal, but simply of public policy to be determined by public advantage. She thought that Mr. Childers had not been popular at the Admiralty and that it was desirable the Secretary for War should be liked by the army. I said that there was an occurrence towards the close of his term which placed him in a difficult position[1] but relied on his care and discretion. (She did not press the point but is evidently under strong professional bias.)

She spoke of the Chancellorship and I named Lord Selborne.

She referred to general action and hoped it would be conciliatory. I said that every one who had served the Crown for even a much smaller term of years than I had the good or ill fortune to reckon would know well that an incoming government must recognise existing engagements and must take up irrespective of its preferences whatever was required by the character and honour of the country. I referred to the case of Scinde and Sir R. Peel's Cabinet in 1843; which she recognised as if it had been recently before her.

---

[1] The replacement of Sir Spencer Robinson as Controller of the Navy by Captain Robert Hall. See ADD MS 44128, ff 160–178, 212–214.

She said I must be frank with you Mr. Gladstone and must fairly say that there have been some expressions, I think she said some little things, which had caused her concern or pain. I said that Her Majesty's frankness so well known was a main ground of the entire reliance of her ministers upon her. That I was conscious of having incurred a great responsibility and felt the difficulty which arises when great issues are raised and a man can only act and speak upon the best lights he possesses, aware all the time that he may be in error. That I had undoubtedly used a mode of speech and language different in some degree from what I should have employed had I been the leader of a party or a candidate for office. Then as regarded conciliation, in my opinion the occasion for what I had described had wholly passed away and that so far as I was concerned it was my hope that Her Majesty would not find anything to disapprove in my general tone: that my desire and effort would be to diminish her cares, in any case not to aggravate them: that, however, considering my years, I could only look to a short term of active exertion and a personal retirement comparatively early.

With regard to the freedom of language I had admitted she said, with some goodnatured archness, 'But you will have to bear the consequences' to which I entirely assented.

She seemed to me, if I may so say 'natural under effort'. All things considered I was much pleased.

I ended by kissing Her Majesty's hand.[1]                    *April 24. 1880.*


**288**  14 May 1880   *Conversation with Musurus Pasha, Turkish Ambassador in London*
ADD MS 56445

*Covering note in secretary's hand* [*to Granville*]
1880  May 13[2]
Mr. Gladstone sends
1. Notes of what he *was to say* to Musurus Pasha.
2. Notes of the actual conversation—and begs that you will kindly return them.

---

[1] For the Queen's account of this audience, see the entry in her journal: *L.Q.V.*, 2nd series, iii. 84–85.
[2] The conversation took place on 14 May.

*WEG's notes for this conversation*

1. Laud the projects of constitution for the provinces (vilayet of Salonica etc.).
2. Idea that in the last resort the Ottoman power is a British interest to be sustained by our arms does *not* form the basis or any part of our policy.
3. We desire the maintenance of the Turkish empire compatibly with the welfare of the people: and think that, where autonomy has been or may be granted, the suzerainty of the Sultan (which would naturally be associated with tribute) might still be useful, and conducive to the peace of Europe.
4. We desire to act in concert with Europe and do not desire the exercise of separate influence.
5. If the arrangement as to Cyprus has produced an idea that we covet Asia Minor or any other territorial acquisition, we not only disclaim any such idea but should regard the acquisition as a misfortune.
6. We view with hope the re-establishment of a Turkish Parliament but
   (a) so that it shall not override any of the concessions made by the Porte to any of the emancipated provinces, or to be so made under the Treaty of Berlin,
   (b) so that the representation be really impartial as between the different religions.
7. That we shall witness with satisfaction any relief which may be legitimately afforded by improved arrangements fiscal or political to the Turkish finances.

*Docketed by WEG:* Sent to G[ranville] and approved. May 13.[1]

*WEG's memorandum of the conversation*

May 14. 1880.
Musurus Pasha called on me. He entered into Turkish history, pitched very high the practical progress and improvements made since the Hattisherif of Gul-Knaneh in 1839; cited Lord Palmerston's statement that Turkey had made more progress than any other country in the

---

[1] Granville replied, 13 May: 'All that you propose to say I concur in, and think very good to be told to Musurus, though I am afraid he will not report it. Is it not a little early to speak of tribute?' (Agatha Ramm, ed., *The Political Correspondence of Mr. Gladstone and Lord Granville 1876–1886*, 2 vols., 1962, i. no. 202).

same time: said that since 1839 England had been thought to have a special interest in the maintenance of the Ottoman Empire: said they could not move too fast but had within themselves great means of improvement: that *autonomies* were *anatomies*, i.e. vivisections of the Empire: that the provinces ought to receive institutions, and that the governors might be appointed for five years; looked forward to a Turkish Parliament and the representation in it of all the provinces not politically emancipated: feared the influence of Russia but still more the plans of Austria: could not recognise the occupation of Bosnia and Herzegovina as an annexation or as other than a temporary arrangement: referred to my having during the former government warned them against contracting loans, and wished they had taken that advice, which he wrote home at the time.

I told him that my union of opinion on foreign affairs with Lord Granville was such that whatever Lord G[ranville] said might be considered as coming from me—that if in my conversations there was anything not in accord with his, it would probably be due to some accidental error on my part.[1]

That I did not feel aware of the existence of a separate and vital English interest in the maintenance of Turkey, but only the interest we had in good order: that I thought Turkey had been, unhappily for herself, led to rely upon the notion that the British nation recognised such an interest and might be depended upon to support her in the last resort.

Yes, he said, Lord Beaconsfield had encouraged that idea and had at the same time done nothing whatever for them—he was glad that our policy was to be substituted for his.

Musurus having referred to the Crimean War as made to sustain this English interest, I said I rather viewed it according to the picture exhibited in the life of the Prince Consort as a war made in support of European legality, which the Czar was endeavouring to infringe in the case of Turkey.

He approved of the idea that the local liberties of the inhabitants of the Balkan Peninsula should not be overshadowed by any foreign influence whatever, and of what I had said about Austria.

---

[1] Argyll wrote to WEG on 20 June 1896: 'Granville's way of conducting foreign affairs was so *quiet*—bringing *as little as possible before the Cabinet* and working chiefly with you alone' (ADD MS 44106, ff 332–333).

I said the Treaty of Berlin was the legal and natural base of our policy—(and he declared Turkey was anxious to give it complete effect): that we did not wish to see separate and special influence exercised in Turkey by other powers, nor by ourselves: that we entertained a sincere good will towards the Empire and desired the supremacy of the Sultan to be maintained, but conditionally upon effective measures for the security and prosperity of the populations, for which the means ought to be efficacious, and the best means would be what we call administrative not political autonomy—with this view the actual tie (lien) ought to be light.

He said that these ideas would give perfect satisfaction to the Porte— the exclusion of foreign influence seemed to be the notion on which he had been instructed to work. He said that Austria had unquestionably entertained the idea of going forward to Salonica.     *May 14. 1880.*

I said as to the Parliament that it ought not to interfere with international arrangements, and that the system of representation ought to be carefully adjusted.

**289**  21 May 1880  *Conversation with Aristarchi Bey, Turkish Attaché at Paris*
ADD MS 56445

Aristarchi Bey called on me today introduced by M. Bylandt.

He said some notable things.

His account of the Sultan agreed in all points with that of Sir H. Layard.

His account of the ministers was still worse.

He hoped the advent of the new government might avail to check and mitigate the descent of Turkey in the scale—assured it could not be—it was the march of history and doom.

He did not found any serious hopes upon a Parliament.

The crying wants of justice, education, finance, could not be supplied by the government.

He saw nothing for it but an international commission, assuming the virtual direction of the empire in these vital matters.

He admitted that the Treaty of Berlin did not go beyond Europe and Armenia: but it would be very much to deal satisfactorily with Europe. (He is a Greek.)

E

He had seen M. Freycinet and found him most cordial towards England.

He (A.B.) thought the renewal of the *entente cordiale* would most effectually promote the settlement of the Turkish question. Germany would favour its plans, at least sentimentally, Russia would not oppose, and the interest of Austria would be to have tranquillity and content upon her borders.

As long as Fuad and Ali were alive he had hopes from them for Turkey—but they had no successors. *May 21. 1880.*

**290** 1 October 1880 *Conversation with Count Münster, German Ambassador in London: the Eastern Question*
ADD MS 56445

Count Münster called on me, unofficially, to ask after my health.

However, we talked on the Eastern Question.

He stated very fully that we had all a common interest in maintaining the concert, and settling the question.

And that it 'seemed impossible' for the six powers to recede before the Turks.

We were alike sensible of the dangers of a general shock to Turkey by making an appearance in the Dardanelles or Bosporus. I said it seemed to me not impossible to arrange for a milder and safer measure of material pressure upon Turkey. He did not give any opinion.

*October 1. 1880.*

**291** 5 May 1882 *Conversation with Captain O'Shea: Parnell and the Irish Party*
ADD MS 44766 ff 71–72

*On 2 May Parnell was released from Kilmainham gaol, agreeing to use his influence against crime and disorder in return for an Arrears Bill.*

Memorandum.
I saw Mr. O'Shea at his request at about six o'clock this evening. He had been up all night, and had long and in his opinion most satisfactory conversation with Parnell who he is confident will carry through what he has intended.

Parnell does not object to the announcement of strong measures in Ireland but is most anxious that they should not be precipitated.

He is confident that the state of Ireland will have greatly improved in a short time. Among the instruments on whose aid he reckons, are Egan and Sheridan. In perfect keeping with what he had reported to Forster he told me that Sheridan was the man who organised the anti-legal agitation throughout Connaught, and who would now be an effectual agent for putting down.

He speaks with the same confidence of Egan.

Mr. O'Shea himself detests and denounces the previous action with regard to outrage.

Parnell much regretted the declarations of Dillon and O'Kelly yesterday during his absence. He also regretted that he had misunderstood my reference to him in consequence of inaccurate information with which *Cowen* supplied him before his actually entering the House.

He considers that he has now got his hand upon Dillon who is difficult to manage and intensely ambitious.

He states that there are great jealousies around him in Parliament: and some men are alarmed at the prospect of losing their livelihood. I am not sure whether this proceeded from O'Shea or from Parnell but I think it seemed as if derived from Parnell, perhaps not as a message.

It is already made known in Ireland that the No Rent manifesto is 'void' and Parnell is anxiously considering what further practical steps he can take with regard to getting formally rid of it.

Parnell *had* communicated with his fellow prisoners before writing his letter to O'Shea.

As nothing can be more clear than that he has used lawlessness for his ends, so O'Shea's statements tend to impress the belief that he is now entirely in earnest about putting it down; but that he feels himself in some danger of being supplanted by more violent men.

O'Shea is to send me the names of some men whom he recommends for early liberation that they may work under Parnell in repressing outrage: I promised to send them to Lord Spencer.

He said he had been up all night: and I do not doubt he has worked hard.                                    *May 5. 1882*

*Docketed by secretary:* 5 May 82. Memorandum. Recording conversation with Mr. O'Shea on Irish situation.

**292** 18 May 1882 *Memorandum by Catherine Gladstone of a conversation with Lady Derby: an invitation to Lord Derby to join the Cabinet*[1]
ADD MS 44766 ff 75–76

My wife's memorandum. May 18.[2]
[3]1882. May 18.
Lady Derby and I had a very friendly and very interesting conversation today. I gathered from it, how they had both felt all the kindness and how deeply interested he and she had been in the offer—seeing an opportunity I tried to bring her out and ventilate the matter. I spoke of the tremendous *difficulties* of the moment, that the offer had come entirely unsought—did not *duty speak in a call like this?* She warmed up and seemed to feel this greatly, and gradually we got more and more as *confiding* in *one another*. I have certainly gathered that *time might* do something. Lady Derby most frankly spoke of her husband's indecision and I left her feeling it would be well worth if possible not to shut the door now—she had been so touched by your last letter she had not dared to shew it to him—he was quite unhappy now. I spoke of the old days when you acted with his father, and if I ventured to say so of the value of acting with one like you and she warmed up still more.

She said the Indian Office was *the* very thing for him. I believe that the being told he must make up his mind at once had a bad effect.

It was upon Lady Derby's speaking of his indecision and the matter being so hurried which led me to say 'Of course I know nothing but if the matter could be delayed say a fortnight by the Chancellor of the Exchequer being kept by my husband.'

**293** 24 May 1882 *Conversation with Lady Derby: a further overture to Lord Derby*
ADD MS 44766 ff 77–80

*Secret.*
I went to Lady Derby's 5 o'clock tea today, with notice, in order to correct a possible misapprehension, and to learn finally whether any door is open in that quarter.

---

[1] See Dudley W. R. Bahlman, ed., *The Diary of Sir Edward Walter Hamilton 1880–1885*, 1972, i. 273–274, for this attempt to persuade Lord Derby to join the Cabinet.
[2] In WEG's hand.
[3] From here onwards in Catherine Gladstone's hand.

In a note, after Lord Derby's negative answer, I had told Lady Derby that I should struggle on as I best could under the burden of my two offices.

After speaking to her on the parliamentary situation, I told her my view was altered, that my mind now inclined to recognise the necessity of a change, and that if the change were made otherwise than by Lord Derby's taking the India Office, I feared it must take a form which would not leave any power of clearing it for his choice hereafter, until some larger alteration of offices should take place, which it was little likely to do unless the improvement of prospects in Ireland, now rendered somewhat uncertain, should enable me to effect my own retirement from office.

I said Lord Hartington was quite ready to take the Exchequer if he was to be succeeded by Lord Derby, but that I could not ask him to quit it to make way for any less prominent and important person.

I assumed that the War Office would under no circumstances be agreable to him, and that he would be unlikely to take the President-ship of the Council, which could be made available.

As to the last, she said Lord Derby had not absolutely renounced it, but she thought he would not like it: as to the War Office, she fully agreed with me: and after an explanation she understood the point about the Exchequer.

She talked variously and uncertainly, on his slowness in decision, and difficulty from haste: thought it would be better probably a short time hence—to which I pointed out the obstacle. She thought he could render more effective support out of office. This I said could not be done except in the case of a minister who had, or believed himself to have, finally retired from the career: such as Lord Grey in the Mel-bourne time, Sir James Graham in the time of the second Palmerston administration, and also Sir R. Peel to Lord John Russell in 1847–50.

She asked how, if the subject were entertained, there could be any move [?]. How much time could be given? Could there be a week?

I replied, that provided the door were open we would find the means of obviating any formal difficulty, on my hearing from her to that effect. That I had been desirous to proceed forthwith but this did not mean before post-time or in a given number of hours: and that a week could be given.

He has a function at Liverpool on Monday and nothing formal could be done in the interim. If she found there was no opening whatever, she would let me know sooner.

I cannot well judge whether there is life in it or not.

*May 24. 1882.*

**294**  11 December 1882  *Audience with the Queen: ministerial appointments*
ADD MS 44766 f 150

December 11.
The subjects at the audience today were[1]
The archbishopric[2]
Arabi and company
Mr. Fawcett
Lord Granville's health and strength
Mr. Childers: all right[3]
Lord Hartington: much approved[4]
Lord Derby          } ἀρρητ ἀρρητων[6]
Sir Charles Dilke[5] } but not hopeless
The subsidiary arrangements—Lord E. Fitzmaurice[7]

*December 11. 1882.*

**295**  7 January 1883  *WEG's health: memorandum for Dr. Clark*[8]
ADD MS 44766 ff 6–7

1. My practice of regulating action by brain.
2. Single sign of brain-resentment heretofore—neuralgia now and then, at the close of the session.

---

[1] WEG consulted Granville before this audience. Ramm (1876–1882), no. 909.

[2] Archbishop Tait had died on 3 December. For the Queen's views on the succession, see Guedalla, ii. no. 930.

[3] To succeed WEG as Chancellor of the Exchequer.

[4] To succeed Childers as Secretary of State for War.

[5] Proposed for Chancellor of the Duchy of Lancaster with a seat in the Cabinet. For the Queen's view, see Guedalla, ii. no. 931.

[6] 'A sin unspeakable'. Sophocles, *Oedipus the King*, l. 465.

[7] To become under-secretary for foreign affairs.

[8] Dr. Andrew Clark, WEG's physician, who visited him on 7 January. For WEG's health in January 1883, and in particular his insomnia, see Ramm (1883–1886), nos. 950, 954, and Hamilton, ii. 384–385.

3. Slight indications of breach in sleep during the autumn sittings.
4. Aggravated since coming here. No notice taken until this week.
5. This week much further aggravation; best night 6 hours, worst (Friday) 2 hours.
6. Some neuralgia in the last three days but not bad.
7. I do not perceive bodily health and functions to be affected, except the brain, which has slight confusion and great sense of weakness all through the day: increase of it today. Beguiled in conversation, but returns. No sleepiness in the day time or evening.
8. During the week I have reduced my transaction of business to the necessary, and given up reading and preparing for my visit to Midlothian. But matters have not improved, indeed the contrary. Light reading however continues to be agreeable to me.

> *Communicated to Dr. Clark on his visit.*
> *Hawarden. Sunday, January 7. 1883.*

**296** January 1883 *'Sleep Register'*[1]
ADD MS 44767 f 1

*On 17 January WEG left for a holiday at Cannes, and returned on 2 March.*

| | | | |
|---|---|---|---|
| At home | Saturday January | 13 | 4 hours |
| At home | Sunday | 14 | 4½ hours |
| | Monday | 15 | 1 hour |
| London | Tuesday | 16 | 5 |
| Train | Wednesday | 17 | 3 |
| Cannes | Thursday | 18 | 8½ |
| | Friday | 19 | 7 |
| | Saturday | 20 | 7 |
| | Sunday | 21 | 7 |
| | Monday | 22 | 6½ |
| | Tuesday | 23 | full 6½ |
| | Wednesday | 24 | 7 |
| | Thursday | 25 | 7½ |
| | Finis | | |

---

[1] WEG's docket.

**297** 31 December 1883  *Conversation with Lord Hartington: Reform and Redistribution*
ADD MS 44767 ff 131–133

*Docketed by WEG:* Memorandum in train to town. December 31. 1883.[1]
Cabinet may postpone whole subject.[2]
Alternatives.
1. Severance of redistribution.
2. Principles of it.
3. *Declaration* of them *now*.
   How as to minority clause?
4. Party. Not disruption
   but dissolution
   with Chamberlain rising *in the distance*.
5. Ireland.
   1. Social.
   2. Political difficulty.
      Party and Parliament. Extreme.
   3. Danger is *none—except* a quarrel, *with Ireland in the right*.

This day Hartington sat with me from 3.15 to 5.45.

I urged upon him first that the Cabinet had not decided on its course with respect to parliamentary reform generally—that the severance of the two branches had been decided on in ignorance of his real sentiments—and that he was bound if he objected to the *contemplated* plan now much expected by the world, to advise an alternative.

I urged principally
a. the ruin to the party, immediately, or else in a short time hence, and the prospect of its re-forming hereafter under extreme auspices,
b. the fearful evil of branding Ireland with political inequality—the only way which could make her really dangerous.
We discussed the particulars of redistribution—as soothingly as I could.
I contended
that to postpone the entire subject to 1885 seemed to be its absolute immolation as I could not see a chance of passing a 'complete measure' in the sixth and last session of a Parliament,

---

[1] ADD MS 44767, f 133. Written in a shaky hand. These are WEG's notes for his conversation with Hartington.
[2] A later addition.

that a wide application of the minority principle in England and Scotland especially in a Franchise Bill and by a Liberal government, was at the present time impossible—would break up all the support of the Bill without conciliating opponents. Such a measure would hardly reach a second reading,

that there could be such application of the principle, in Ireland, unless it were also applied to England and Scotland.[1]

*Docketed by secretary:* December 1883. Memorandum of interview with Lord Hartington.

**298** 10–30 March 1884 *Cabinet meetings on the Sudan*
ADD MS 56451

Cabinet.

From the 10th onwards until 30th I was forbidden to attend Cabinets. They were held on (Tuesday) 11th, 13th, 15th, 16th and other days: communication held with me in various degrees by envoys. On Saturday 15th it seemed as if by my casting vote Zobeir was to be sent to Gordon. The division of opinion is noted by Granville on one of the memoranda within.[2] But on Sunday the Chancellor and Chamberlain receded from their ground, and I gave way. The nature of the evidence, on which judgments are formed in this most strange of all cases, precludes (in reason) pressing all conclusions, which are but preferences, to extremes.

March 30. I resumed.

**299** 13 November 1884 *Conversation with Sir Stafford Northcote: Reform and Redistribution*
ADD MS 44768 ff 146–147

Early.
Lord Granville
Lord Hartington.[3]

---

[1] See also Hamilton, ii. 535, and Ramm (1883–1886), no. 1202.

[2] Among related papers (ADD MS 56451) is a pencilled note in Granville's hand, recording that Derby, the Chancellor, Hartington, Chamberlain, Dodson, Carlingford and WEG himself were for sending Zobeir, and Granville, Harcourt, Northbrook, Kimberley, Dilke and Childers against.

[3] The memorandum is marked as having been seen by both Granville and Hartington.

In consequence of a communication from Mr. Northcote to Mr. West, Sir Stafford Northcote and I met late last night at Mr. West's.

We agreed that the conversation should be *secret*, and I assured him that within these four walls I should speak to him with the freedom of entire confidence.

The sum of our conversation was I think as follows.

1. I placed in his hands the query which is written within[1] having copied it for the purpose.
2. I told him that I saw no advantage in exchange of views except in order to procure the passing of the Franchise Bill peacefully and forthwith.
3. I did not see any objection to our making known our views *in extenso*, and even if requisite in the form of a draft Bill; nor in our engaging to make the Bill, especially as to any enactments which might be the basis of any understanding, a vital question.
4. On the question of procedure, he saw difficulties in my Query and evidently leaned to delay, which I shut out, but said we should not object to proceed with a Redistribution Bill before Christmas.
5. On the subject matter of Redistribution he was most satisfactory: he made no *sine quâ non:* was moderate on severance of rural and urban elements: admitted the great objections to grouping in important classes of cases: was not averse to one-member districts: and did not much cling to the minority vote.
6. He will answer me, first seeing Salisbury.

*November 13–14. 1884. 1 a.m.*

A Cabinet today would probably be premature?

*Note by Granville:* It is sad to say, but if you had one you could not rely on secrecy.   G.

---

[1] ADD MS 44768, f 137. It is docketed by WEG 'No. 1. Copy of Query placed in the hands of Sir S. Northcote by Mr. Gladstone at a private conversation on the night of November 13. 1884, which he proposed to communicate to Lord Salisbury.' It reads: 'Secret. What assurances will you require about the character of our Redistribution Bill, as a condition of engaging that, if we produce it before the Franchise Bill reaches the Committee in the Lords, and make it a vital question, the Franchise Bill shall there be put forward without difficulty or delay? November 13. 1884.' WEG's Cabinet circular of 13 November, proposing this course of action, is ADD MS 44645, ff 203–204. Agreement was eventually reached at a series of meetings between 19 and 27 November.

**300** 16–22 June 1885  *WEG's resignation and the formation of Lord Salisbury's Ministry*
ADD MSS 44769 ff 129–132, 135–136, 138–144, 154–155, 167–168; 44491 ff 122–125

*The crisis began on 9 June, when WEG resigned after a defeat on the Budget, and lasted until 23 June, when through the mediation of the Queen Lord Salisbury agreed to form a ministry. Salisbury had been advised that a dissolution of Parliament was impossible until a general election could be held on the new register in the new constituencies. He therefore attempted to extract specific pledges regarding supply etc. from WEG, but had eventually to content himself with general assurances that the Liberals would not embarrass the new minority government on vital financial questions.*

*Documents relating to those printed below are to be found in Add MS 44769 (ff 137, 145–149, 156–180) and MS Loan 73/24 (Gladstone Royal Correspondence, including a note on the events of 22 June). See also Morley, iii. 202–208, and Guedalla, ii. 361–375.*

16 June 1885   *Conversation with Arthur James Balfour*[1]
No. 1[2]

June 16.

Mr. Balfour called, on the part of his uncle, soon after one. He wished to know:

(1) whether I should be prepared to support Lord Salisbury's government in giving preference to supply, and to ways and means—on all days when they might be put down as first order;

(2) whether if the government made financial proposals and I disapproved them, I would support raising the money by exchequer bills.

I said the questions were very pointed and peculiar, and not such as I could have anticipated.

I referred to the communications of December 1845 between Lord J. Russell and Sir R. Peel—and gave him the *Memoir*[3] for reference.

---

[1] ADD MS 44769, ff 129–131.

[2] This is the first of a series of documents, originally enclosed in a cover docketed by WEG: 'Resignation of 1885.' The others are printed below.

[3] *Memoirs by Sir Robert Peel*, ed. Stanhope and Cardwell, 2 vols., 1856, 1857, vol. ii.

I told him:

(1) that I was not prepared to depart from the mode then pursued as to the initiative which I conceived to have lain with the Queen: that such inquiries would have to be presented in writing;

(2) that if there were any question of an understanding or covenant, I conceived (especially after the recent confidential and peculiar arrangement) that it must be made public;

(3) that if the questions he had reported were put to me, it would be necessary for me to consult with others upon them.

He asked if he might send me the questions unofficially and as from himself that I might have them before me.

I told him that this might economise time, and I had no objection. He went away. *June 16. 1885.*

16 June 1885    *A. J. Balfour to WEG*[1]

I have communicated your views to Lord Salisbury; and he entirely concurs with the opinion you expressed, that any arrangement made between the outgoing and the incoming ministers should be of a public character, and that the Queen is the constitutional channel through which all communication between the two parties should be made.

This letter therefore is to be taken as merely from myself, and as written in deference to a suggestion you made at the interview you were good enough to give me this morning.

The two points on which I ventured to say that it was important that some arrangement should be come to, in view of the very exceptional circumstances in which a Conservative government (should such be formed) would find itself at the present juncture were these:

First, in regard the time of the House, that no difficulty should be made in giving precedence to government business whether supply or ways and means was put down first order of the day.

Secondly, that, if such financial proposals as we might make should prove unacceptable to the majority of the House, the opposition should not object to government raising, by the issue of exchequer bonds, the money which may be required to meet the estimates and vote of credit brought in by the late administration.

I fully admit the accuracy of your statement this morning that for an incoming administration to make a request for support of this very

---

[1] ADD MS 44491, ff 122–125.

definite and precise character to an outgoing administration is wholly without precedent. The sole justification for such a course lies in the fact that it is also without precedent that a Prime Minister should not find himself in a position of perfect freedom with regard to advising Her Majesty to dissolve Parliament.

I return Sir R. Peel's *Memoir* with many thanks.

16 June 1885  *Draft of WEG's reply to A. J. Balfour*[1]
No. 2. It was thought upon receiving the enclosed (no. 3)[2] that I might reply as follows.
A [*First draft, deleted.*]
June 16. Substitute for A.
In the conduct of the necessary business of the country there will I believe be no disposition to embarrass the government of the Queen but I do not think it would be for the public advantage that I should enter upon specific pledges.

18 June 1885  *Conversation with the Queen*[3]
Circulate.
While I was at Windsor today there came a telegram from Lord Salisbury stating that in the unanimous opinion of his friends my declaration was of no value.

I had a full conversation with the Queen who was very gracious, and appeared to attach weight to many things that I said—for example as to the strange position in which we and the House would be placed were we to give the assurances he requested.

She requested me to put down some heads to assist her memory, which I did in her presence.

One to which she attached value, as it seemed, ran nearly as follows.

'In my opinion the whole value of any such declaration as the present circumstances permit really depends upon the spirit in which it is given and taken. For myself, and for any friend of mine I can only say that the spirit in which we should endeavour to interpret and apply the declaration I have made would be the same spirit in which we entered upon the recent conferences concerning the Seats Bill.'

A copy of these documents will be sent me.

*June 18. 1885.*

---

[1] ADD MS 44769, f 132. In WEG's hand.
[2] Balfour to WEG, 16 June.
[3] ADD MS 44769, ff 135–136.

'*Memorandum submitted by Mr. Gladstone to Her Majesty at Windsor. June 18. 1885*'[1]

1. Can Lord Salisbury suggest any amendment to my words which would make them satisfactory?
2. In my opinion the whole value of such a declaration as circumstances like these admit depends upon the spirit in which it is given and received. For myself and for any friends of mine I can only say that we give the declaration, and should endeavour to interpret and apply it, in the same spirit in which we entered upon the recent conferences on the Seats Bill.
3. I am of opinion that it would be easy to convince Lord Salisbury himself that it is entirely beyond our power to give the specific pledges which he requires.
4. I can confidently say that so far as my knowledge goes there is not the slightest intention to make an extreme or illegitimate use of the power of a majority—were it in our power so to do.
5. About the dissolution, on the facts before us, there is no difference of opinion.

(signed) WEG 18 June 1885

*c*18 June 1885    *WEG's statement of the constitutional position*[2]

1. I have endeavoured in my letters
(a) to avoid all controversial matter,
(b) to consider not what the incoming ministers had a right to ask, but what it was possible for us, in a spirit of conciliation, to give.
2. In our opinion there was no right to demand from us anything whatever. The declarations we have made represent an extreme of concession.

The conditions required, e.g. the first of them, place in abeyance the liberties of Parliament by leaving it solely and absolutely in the power of the ministers to determine on what legislative or other questions (except supply) it shall be permitted to give a judgment.

House of Commons may and ought to be disposed to facilitate the progress of all necessary business by all reasonable means as to supply and otherwise but would deeply resent any act of ours by which we agreed beforehand to the proposed extinction of its discretion.

---

[1] Ibid., ff 167–168. Copy, in secretary's hand.
[2] Ibid., ff 154–155.

The difficulties pleaded by Lord Salisbury were all in view when his political friend Sir M. H. Beach made the motion which as we apprised him would if carried eject us from office, and are simply the direct consequences of their own action.

If it be true that Lord Salisbury loses the legal power to advise, and the Crown to grant, a dissolution, that cannot be a reason for leaving in the hands of the executive an absolute power to stop the action (except as to supply) of the legislative and corrective power of the House of Commons. At the same time these conditions do not appear to me to attain the end proposed by Lord Salisbury: for it would still be left in the power of the House to refuse supplies and thereby to bring about in its worst form the difficulty which he apprehends.

20 June 1885   *Visit from Sir Henry Ponsonby*[1]
3 p.m. June 20.
Ponsonby has been with me. He has delivered my letter to Salisbury.

He does not know when the next turn of the wheel will come.

1. Query. Can the Queen do anything more?
I answered. As you ask me, it occurs to me that it might help Salisbury's going on were she to make reference to no. 2 of my memorandum. And to say that in her judgment he would be safe in receiving it in a spirit of trust.
2. Query. If Lord Salisbury fails may the Queen rely on you?
I answered that on a previous day I had said that if Salisbury failed the situation would be altered. I hoped, and on the whole thought, he would go on. But if he did not? I could not promise or expect smooth water—the movement of questions such as Crimes Act, and Irish local government might be accelerated. But my desire would be to do my best to prevent the Queen's being left without a government.   *June 20.*

22 June 1885   *Interviews with Sir Henry Ponsonby*[2]
June 22. 1885.
Sir H. Ponsonby brought to me Lord Salisbury's letter to the Queen dated June 20.

[*Two or three words over-written and unintelligible*] that it was written before my letter of yesterday, and learning that my letter of yesterday

---

[1] Ibid., ff 138–139.
[2] Ibid., ff 140–144.

had been shown to Lord Salisbury who had not as yet made any observation upon it, I said that there was nothing for me to do at present, as I was not aware whether Lord Salisbury's whole view of the present facts was before me.

Sir Henry Ponsonby went off to Lord Salisbury and returned before half past one.

He stated that Lord Salisbury was struck by the paragraph relating to facilities for supply, and by the paragraph relating to ways and means—if he might assume that they being contained in a reply to a letter of Her Majesty, and not written in answer to him, would form part of the public chain of correspondence.

I said they were absolutely at Her Majesty's disposal.

Sir Henry Ponsonby asked would it be well for Her Majesty to recommend Lord Salisbury to accept them?

I said I saw no objection. *June 22. 1885. 2 p.m.*

At 3 p.m. Sir Henry Ponsonby brought me a draft of what Her Majesty might possibly write to Lord Salisbury for my approval. I pointed out objections to parts of it—notably to passages omitting the necessity of assurances—and stating that my two paragraphs were substantially for practical purposes what Lord Salisbury required.

I said I could not be a party to any interpretation of the paragraphs— or to more than the Queen's giving her judgment that Lord Salisbury might reasonably accept these paragraphs. *June 22. 3.20 p.m.*

See A within
    B ditto.

A. June 22. 85.

At about a quarter past four, Sir H. Ponsonby returned hither [10 Downing Street] for his fourth [*sic*] interview of today.

Lord Salisbury was not he said satisfied with the draft in which the Queen might (so ran the plan) assure him that in her opinion he might reasonably accept the two paragraphs in my letter of June 21: but required to be added to them certain words which I had struck out, as impossible to be sent with my privity or participation. These words ran somewhat as follows: 'as conveying for all practical purposes the substance of what he had required'.

Through these words I had drawn my pencil. *June 22. 85. 4¾ p.m.*

B. June 22.

At 5.40 Sir H. Ponsonby returned for a fifth [*sic*] interview, his infinite patience not yet exhausted.

He brought from Lord Salisbury another version of the supposed Queen's letter which after saying that in Her Majesty's opinion Lord Salisbury might reasonably rely on the two paragraphs went on in terms like these:

'as convincing and adequate assurance of such support as is necessary to enable the new government to carry through the necessary business of the remainder of the session'.

I said that without presuming to interfere with what Her Majesty might think proper to write I must own that I could not in any way be party to words of this kind, or place any interpretation on the paragraphs of June 21.

He said the Queen believed that the late government did not wish to come back.

I simply reminded him of my previous replies, which he remembered nearly as follows:

That if Lord Salisbury failed the situation would be altered.

That I could not in such case promise Her Majesty smooth water.

That however, a great duty in such circumstances lay upon any one holding my situation, to use his best efforts so as, *quoad* what depended upon him, not to leave the Queen without a government. I think he will now go to Windsor.                    *June 22. 85. 6 p.m.*


**301** 30 January–6 February 1886 *The formation of WEG's third Ministry*[1]
ADD MS 44771 ff 29–33, 46–47, 51–52, 57, 60, 62

January 30. 1886.[2] Begun 10.30 a.m.
Summoned various persons by note: especially Hartington–James.
1. Saw Granville. Spencer summoned—letter dispatched. Derby. Granville to see him. Invite between 12 and 1. Wrote to Sydney.
2. R. Grosvenor. List. He will see F. Leveson.

---

[1] See also Appendix 2.
[2] ADD MS 44771, ff 29–33.


F                                                                                73

3. Hartington—explained motives—and friendliness. I asked him to write his negative and reasons.

4. Sir H. James. My strong insistence. Difficulty on his side, election pledges. I said do not relieve yourself at the expense of the public interest. He said, I cannot go back to Bury. I said, we may find you another seat. Come again.

5. Lord Wolverton. Seat for James?

6. Sir J. Pauncefote. Brought cipher. Learnt position of the question of Greek fleet.

7. Lord Derby—friendly negative. Too much committed by opposite declarations heretofore. Communicates with Hartington. Has much the same feelings.

8. Sir H. Ponsonby. Osborne on Monday. Reported fully to him all I have done thus far.

Late Cabinet 16 [members]. see A.[1] Five gone, two uncertain, nine counted on. Mentioned possible men. Ripon, Morley, Mundella, Campbell-Bannerman, Courtney. (Wolverton not mentioned) nor Bright. Probably small.

9. Wolverton. Report. Seat for James.

10. Lord Granville. Will write to Duke of Westminster. Will see Harcourt and inform him of my action today. Approves Admiralty for Chamberlain.

11. Mr. Primrose—to be a private secretary. Details reserved.

12. Chamberlain. Could not agree to Irish programme without union. This he practically withdrew. 'Liberty of rejection and judgment is unlimited, consideration of minor plans is not excluded.' Freely agreed to.

Will send answer. Talked of Dilke and Foreign Office. I said, 'I have undertaken an immense responsibility and I must endeavour to go through with it though my difficulties may increase from day to day.' It looked like yes.

12a. Granville present at the latter part, and very useful. He reported about Harcourt.

13. Mr. Hamilton—to see Godley as to Primrose.

14. Lord Richard Grosvenor reporting respecting Lord Granville, and on F. Leveson about him.

15. Lord Selborne. Explanations. Friendly negative.

---

[1] ADD MS 44771, ff 63–64. 'Government of 1885 as it stood on resigning'.

16. Mr. Chamberlain brought his acceptance. I suggested amendments which he will incorporate. Wishes Colonies rather than Admiralty? Hopes Mr. Collings will have an office with re-election.
17. Mr. Childers at 7.20. Accepts War. Detailed to him all main particulars. Showed Irish memorandum[1] to him as well as to
    Sir Henry Ponsonby
    Mr. Chamberlain
    Lord Granville
    Derby
    Hartington
    Sir H. James
and substance to Lord Selborne.
18. Lord Spencer. At my disposal for any office or none.
    I said, some, absolutely.
    The rest stands over.
    He will see F. Leveson about [*unfinished*]

Sunday, January 31. 1886.[2]
1. Sir F. Herschell to come at one.
   Saw Methuen having inquired basis: I explained it: quite satisfied: accepts.
2. John Morley two p.m. All in the right sense. Asks until *near six*.
3. Arnold Morley half past two: accepts.
4. To Ponsonby: E. W. Hamilton will telegraph my arrival.
5. To Beach: Lord Richard Grosvenor will see him and ask adjournment to Thursday.
6. Lord R. Grosvenor. To see Granville about Duke of Westminster.
7. E. W. Hamilton. Primrose to be first private secretary.
8. Saw Granville. He did not name the subject. Was grave. We spoke of Chamberlain and Herschell.
9. Chamberlain's acceptance arrived say at three.
10. Wolverton thought Granville might be First Lord and I Chancellor of Exchequer. I did not exclude this at once but wrote to him on it.
11. Saw Harcourt—previously seen by Hamilton at my desire. He despaired and made difficulties—agreed with Chamberlain and with Hartington—hoped Cabinet would be *free* to consider

---

[1] ADD MS 44771, ff 44–45.
[2] Ibid., ff 46–47.

question of an Irish legislative body either way. But came in and would not refuse office.

12. Childers. Reported conversation with Hartington.
13. Morley—stated objections to himself—but accepted.
14. Spencer—nothing to report from Granville. We went over all the ground. He had my assent to his saying that after full conversation I was confident he would do wisely to accept an office other than the Foreign Office which no one had ever taken at his age. I told him *secretly* the opinion of Herschell and James.
15. Hamilton, about to dine with F. Leveson, authorised to speak similarly to him.

February 3. 1886.[1]
1. Saw Trevelyan—settled.
2. Sir H. Ponsonby—we move on. He returns at 2.45.
3. Lord Richard Grosvenor as to G. Leveson.
4. Sir J. Carmichael. Second private secretary.
5. Campbell-Bannerman—yes—showed memorandum.
6. G. Leveson—yes.
7. Richard Grosvenor respecting Wolverton.
8. Wolverton. I hope. His wish to leave the incidents of office to others.
   Why not Morley for Works?
   Office to Kim[berley] [?].
9. Goschen. Conversation on J. Collings's motion and on Ireland. He has seen Hartington's letter. Did not say he agreed.
10. Conclave at Granville's.
11. Mundella—settled.
12. Viceroy of Ireland. 1. Camperdown.
                        2. Dalhousie.
                        3. Aberdeen.
12a. Wrote to Playfair.
13. Works. Morley—with G. Leveson in House of Commons.
14. Attorney-General C. Russell.
15. Admiralty. Brassey [*deleted*].
16. Ripon—Morley (earl)—Kimberley—accept. ditto C. Russell.

---

[1] Ibid., ff 51–52.

17. Notes to Fowler—Treasury—Secretary.
    *Kay Shuttleworth—India
    *Hibbert—Admiralty Secretary
    * under cover to chief.
    Balfour Lord Advocate
    O. Morgan Judge Advocate
    Duff Civil Lord Admiralty
    Asher Solicitor-General Scotland.
18. To see Kenmare—Marjoribanks—Cyril Flower.

February 4. 1886.[1]
1. Sir L. Playfair accepts.
2. Lord R. Grosvenor—gave him my address[2] to read.
3. Lord Kenmare—offer his old office—explanation. To return at one.
4. Richard Grosvenor and Rosebery. On my address: they approve. Also on Bryce.
5. Hibbert to be Secretary Admiralty with Privy Council.
6. Broadhurst to be Secretary Board of Trade.
7. O. Morgan. Judge Advocate.
8. Fowler to be Secretary Treasury.
9. Herbert J. Gladstone in War Office probably Financial Secretary.
10. Wolverton to be Postmaster-General.
11. Kenmare to be Chamberlain.
12. Cyril Flower Lord of Treasury.
13. Craig Sellar ditto—contingent [?].
14. Heneage the Duchy.
15. Stuart Rendell—started for Colonial Office under-Secretary.
16. Marjoribanks Controller of the Household.
17. Six recommendations sent to Queen by post.

February 5. 1886.[3]
1. Saw Lord Granville. Viceroyalty etc.
2. Lord Richard Grosvenor and Arnold Morley—preparation of estimates—offices discussed.

---

[1] Ibid., f 57.
[2] His address to the electors of Midlothian: draft, ibid., ff 53–56; fair copy, ibid., ff 68–71.
[3] Ibid., f 60.

3. Herbert Gladstone to choose.
4. Conclave.
Ireland—Home Office—proposals to Collings
                              Aberdeen
                              Reed—Lord Treasury
                              Broadhurst—under-Secretary
                              Home

February 6. 1886.[1]
My colleagues went to Osborne.
Saw Lord Granville
    Lord Richard Grosvenor
    Mr. A. Morley
    Private secretary.
Operations chiefly concerned Surveyorship
                           Household
                           Sir C. Reed Lordship
and arrangements with a view to writs.
Closing day's work here.

**302**  16 March 1886  *Memorandum on a letter of rebuke from the Queen*
ADD MS 44772 f 1

Secret.
After this letter of rebuke from the Queen[2] had caused me to write two long letters to Her Majesty on the subject,[3] I learnt with surprise that the Queen when she wrote it had not read my speech[4] but only a summary of it which proved to be incorrect!

    No schoolmaster could govern a school on such principles.

    There has been no expression of regret. A Queen—most unhappily for her—can no more confess, than a journalist.    *March 16. 1886.*

---

[1] Ibid., f 62.

[2] Guedalla, ii. no. 1287 (6 March).

[3] Ibid., ii. nos. 1288 (6 March) and 1290 (8 March). See also the Queen's letter of 7 March (ibid., no. 1289).

[4] 5 March, on Labouchere's motion against hereditary representation (*Parliamentary Debates*, 3rd series, cciii. 44–49).

**303** 17 May 1886 *Conversation with Sir Henry Ponsonby: the progress of the Home Rule Bill*
ADD MS 44772 ff 111–117

*Secret.*

Sir H. Ponsonby called on me today to inquire on the part of Her Majesty, whether I could give her any light as to what was likely to follow the division on the second reading of the Irish Government Bill.

I said that there was so much matter seething and simmering, and so much of uncertainty whether it would come to anything, that I could say but little, though it was probable in two or three days I might be able to form something more like a forecast.

The balance of chances in the present circumstances was against the Bill, but modes of proceeding had been suggested, and appeared to be desired, by a fringe of the opponents, and by a fringe of our supporters, which might if adopted carry the Bill through the second reading.

One suggestion, which had been made by a friend, and to which a certain number of intending opponents had given their adhesion, was that the Bill, after being read a second time should be postponed until the autumn or a new Bill then brought in. This idea was still in agitation.

Sir Henry Ponsonby might acquaint Her Majesty that viewing the contents of the Bill we had arrived at the conclusion that, if fair allowance be made for adequate discussion, it would not be possible to carry the measure within the ordinary limits of the session, as it could not go to the House of Lords until the month of August was running.

I told him that in my judgment a reasonable adjustment of the question respecting the attendance of the Irish Members in Parliament might be arrived at so as to maintain the common concern of the countries in imperial matters but I gave this as my own opinion only and said it was clearly impossible for the government, when the suggestions it had already made were met by malcontents with a cold and unfriendly reception, to put out new suggestions with loss of dignity and, presuming the same temper to exist, no hope of profit.

Sir Henry Ponsonby said as from himself, there seemed to be good sense in an idea expressed by Lord Penzance that if the union were really preserved the difficulty would be removed.

I said it became a question of terms and their interpretation. I conceived that the union is maintained in essence by the Bill as it stands, but our duty was to consider anxiously even the unfounded jealousies of persons favourable to our real views; we had therefore sought to exhibit this union more fully by the amendments we had proffered, and it would be our duty to act further in that sense if the way could be opened without prejudice to the aim of the Bill.

I did not explain to him what I had referred to as a reasonable adjustment.

He said—and to say this was not improbably a main part of his purpose in calling on me—that I might have heard statements to the effect that the Queen would refuse us the power of dissolution should we advise it. There was not a word of truth in them: she had said nothing of the kind.

I answered that I had not heard such statements beyond this that Lord R. Churchill confidently expected Her Majesty would take that course—I could well conceive that Her Majesty had not found occasion to say anything on the subject but I should have given no credence to such statements had I heard them.

The advice to be given might depend on other circumstances than the aye or no of the division, for instance the smallness of the majority might affect it. It was of course the duty of the government while making every allowable effort to conciliate yet upon failure of such efforts to be firm in perseverance.

I referred to the extraordinary speech of Lord Salisbury on Saturday,[1] but this was antecedently to the main conversation.[2]

*May 17. 1886.*

**304** 5 April 1887 *Conversation with Joseph Chamberlain: Irish policy*[3]
ADD MS 44773 ff 35–38

*WEG's notes for this conversation*[4]
Avoid all retrospective discussion and regret.
From whom should he and I have 'full powers'?
*Between us and the two senior questions stands coercion.*

---

[1] *The Times*, 17 May.
[2] For Ponsonby's report to the Queen of this conversation, see George Earle Buckle, ed., *The Letters of Queen Victoria*, Third series, 1930–1932, i. 130.
[3] For this meeting, and Chamberlain's memorandum of the conversation, see C. H. D. Howard, ed., *A Political Memoir, 1880–1892*, 1953, 262–268.
[4] ADD MS 44773, ff 37–38.

Had always hoped we might find here a common ground.

Our line is taken.

Coercion further complicated by *closure*.

Glad to agree on the *new rule*.

Is the rule against alteration of it absolute? If not could not *its Ayes* promote change?

As to arrangements the mischief lay in the announcement as to *second reading before Easter*.

A conference *now* would be dangerous.

Do our best from time to time—according to circumstances.

*Supposing* Mr. Chamberlain were inclined to suggest the exclusion of the Speaker from the closure rule, would his doing it, or being known to desire and be ready to promote it, be well or ill taken by our friends?

Randolph Churchill thought Parnell's demand wholly reasonable *except* for want of sufficient notice.

*WEG's memorandum of the conversation*[1]

Chamberlain

has plenty of qualms on coercion

finds John Bright has none

agrees it is a good question for us, bad for them, with the country.

His anxiety to bring round table to a result was because he saw coercion must greatly widen the breach.

(a)[2] Supposes (but asks if) I think coercion now occupies the ground and precludes further prosecution of the Home Rule and land purchase discussions.

He himself is very nearly of that opinion—not disposed to dispute it.

Sees that the bulk of his wing will be destroyed at the next election.

Remains of opinion there *must* be a settlement and a large settlement of the question.

His course open in regard to particulars of coercion—and thinks the same of the wing.

Dark anticipations for the future of the party which will have increased difficulty in holding up against the Tories.

Can never be a Tory, but the wing on the Hartington side will join the Tories.

---

[1] ADD MS 44773, ff 35–36.
[2] Added later in margin.

Hartington has certainly been moving away from the Liberals.

He and James could readily agree upon a concession in the matter of Irish government by formulating what they think might and ought to be given—fears Parnell would denounce it at once.

Hartington not desirous to give anything, might agree for a great purpose.

Agrees about *closure* that the present intervention of the Speaker is mischievous and ought to be got rid of.

(b)[1] Fears *his* mixing in the matter would be resented by our friends.

I said I would inquire on *a* and *b*.                    *April 5. 1887.*

I said I hoped the bill would be mitigated in its passage—though best for us, in a party sense, as it is.

He admitted coercion was a bad ground for them in the country.

He referred to his going out of Parliament as an alternative if Toryism dominates.

**305**  25 May 1887  *Conversation with Sir George Otto Trevelyan: retention of Irish Members at Westminster*
ADD MS 44773 ff 41–42

*Secret.*
May 25. Conversation with Trevelyan.

Trevelyan dined here last night and we conversed on the subject of my letter.[2] He 'agreed with the whole of it' but would much prefer my speaking it, to its appearing as addressed to him, which he thought would diminish its effect. Especially he desired the concluding portion about Hartington to be known.

Strong on the necessity of speech at this time, and sanguine as to the disposition of the party to reunion, except as regards the mass of the dissentients in the House of Commons who he thinks have no such desire, he also felt it was unreasonable to call on me at this juncture to propound methods of altering and improving the Bill of last year. He

---

[1] Added later in margin.
[2] See below.

thinks however that the desire for the retention of Irish Members is very general. (Lady Spencer spoke in the same sense, West in the opposite.)

I told him of Macknight (*Northern Whig*) who expressed a very strong opinion the other way and of the utter insecurity not to say more, of a committal to a plan without a clear idea of the mode for working it out; also I thought there was no uniform idea or plan even in the minds of those who called for the retention. He pleaded with justice that the average man was not well informed as to the scope of what had been already conceded, while he was perplexed or perverted by Chamberlain's unwarrantable assertions. He commented strongly on the dissentient organisation.

I told him I had been thinking what I could contribute to the work of reunion outside (despairing within doors). Home Rule had already been put out of view for a length of time by coercion.

My opinion is as follows.

The supremacy of Parliament being secure, there is but one essential point namely that a real and effective autonomy should be conceded to Ireland.

Can I safely say that, provided this condition be attained, I am of opinion that any plan for it ought to be accepted and promoted, or that it ought not to be set aside on account of its containing other faulty provisions for example provisions which might entail inconvenience (in my opinion) within the British Parliament, as that body would be sure to feel the mischief and would be free to apply a remedy.

If I said this I should reserve my own freedom as to proposing such a plan but should declare in favour of accepting and promoting it.

I understood him to say he thought this would cover everything. In fact he appeared to be greatly satisfied with the conversation. I said I would make up my mind before going to Wales whether I would speak in the sense I had described: but my present inclination was that way.

*May 26. 1887.*

What I threw out to Trevelyan was in accordance with a memorandum made on the 24th.[1]

---

[1] ADD MS 44773, ff 39–40. Docketed by WEG: 'Memorandum sent to Mr. Morley'. See also WEG to Morley, 28 May 1887, ADD MS 44255, ff 201–202.

*WEG to Sir George Otto Trevelyan, Dollis Hill, [24 May 1887]*[1]

The course which you have pursued with reference to the present proposal to legislate against combination in Ireland under the name of legislating against crime, entitles you to the warm acknowledgements of Liberals; and in your recent speeches you have evidently approached the question of reunion within the party in a spirit of candour and equity.

I have already given proofs of my desire to amend, wherever it may be practicable, the plans for giving effect to the policy of Home Rule in Ireland, which were submitted by the government of February 1886. But a long experience in parliamentary legislation makes me aware that nothing could be less conducive to the end in view than to undertake in our present circumstances to give an account in a working form, of what may eventually be practicable and proper. I may, however, observe that I entered into imperative engagements on behalf of the government, at a time when we were in a position to redeem any promises we made. This was in the debate on the second reading of the Irish Government Bill. The dates were on the [10th of May and 7th of June] and the passages relating to the retention of Irish Members at Westminster will be found at [pp. 23–25, and p. 6 of the respective speeches. Those passages did not exclude, but rather implied, further reflection on the subject.]

I wish further to contribute what I can, towards clearing from ambiguity a question on which so much depends, by a brief statement, under two heads, of my own personal duty and intention with regard to it. On the one hand, I can never be responsible for recommending to the people of Ireland, as a measure of Home Rule, any plan except one which shall combine a real and effective autonomy in Irish concerns with the unquestioned supremacy of Parliament. On the other hand, I will not stand in the way of the adoption of any inferior, that is to say more contracted, plan, if it contain elements of clear and substantial good, and if it be truly desired by the Irish nation. I do not at present see what further security I can give against becoming in my own person an obstacle to a settlement, which beyond all other political objects I desire.

You have seemed to suggest that there should be some communica-

---

[1] ADD MS 44335, ff 216–217. Copy, not in WEG's hand. Interpolations by WEG are within square brackets.

tion between Lord Hartington and myself, or as it has been thought by some, between Lord Hartington and some other person in my place whom public reasons might recommend for the purpose. When last I communicated with Lord Hartington on Irish affairs, I understood him to decline binding himself to agree [(quite apart from the question about Ulster)] to the establishment on whatever conditions of any central body entitled to act for Ireland. Perhaps I misunderstood him, [still] you will see that, with this impression on my mind, it is not for me to propose to him at present a further conference on Irish affairs. But I wish to say that, on his giving any intimation of a desire for such a conference, I should rejoice either to enter upon, or [to] promote it, by every means in my power.

**306**  *post* 8 June 1887   *Comments on a letter by Professor Tyndall: WEG and Home Rule*
ADD MS 44773 ff 46–47

*On 8 June 1887 Professor John Tyndall wrote in a letter to* The Times *about WEG's Home Rule proposals: 'A former worshipper of the ex-Prime Minister said to me some time ago: "Never in the history of England was there such a consensus of intellect arrayed against a statesman as that now arrayed against Mr. Gladstone. What a fall!" I rejoice to find this unanimity of judgment so specially illustrated among scientific men. Trained in the veracities of nature, they have with few exceptions, small tolerance for the sophistries of the English Home Rule leader.'[1] In reply, WEG wrote the following memorandum, which appears never to have been published.*

And so says Professor Tyndall there is a marvellous combination (reporting the observation of some one evidently as wise as himself) or 'consensus of intellect now arrayed against Mr. Gladstone'. There are two sides to that question, as a question of fact. But I take the boaster at his own modest estimate of himself and of his friends. And I do not disparage intellect, but am tempted sometimes to worship it, and have paid it the best practical homage in my power by endeavours greater than those of most other men to extend [?] and to enlarge the very moderate stock of it with which I began life. Intellect is a grand and imposing power without which the world would sink to chaos. But it is not more important than other elements of our state with which it may

---

[1] There is a press cutting of Tyndall's letter at f 45.

be associated or from which it may be divorced. Professor Tyndall among his other boasts has this that they are 'trained in the veracities of nature', veracities (to use a questionable phrase) for which I have an infinite respect. But does his boast mean that he has been trained in pursuits which do not train nor touch the emotions and the affections, nor human sympathies, nor the deeper interests of life, nor the great human brotherhood? If so then they must go a little beyond their own boundaries in order to integrate their education: and must not, as I am confident most of them do not, suppose that they have a monopoly of intellect. Some of it for example was left for Shakespeare. But intellect does not stand alone. The purpose for which we were sent into this world was I apprehend to increase the good and to diminish the sorrow that are in it: and speaking now as the Professor speaks about the world of human action, I am not sure that the great changes and advancements, which made the renown of the present century, have been produced by intellect so much or nearly so much as by moral causes. It was not for want of intellect that France drew upon herself the French Revolution: the action of her great men of the seventeenth century lies at the root of her worst calamities. It was not for want of intellect, but in the full blaze of its splendour, that Italy, especially, fell into a condition which made the tremendous convulsions of the Reformation a necessity for the life of Christendom. If these are facts perhaps Professor Tyndall may admit them into the rank of veracities. But whether he does or not, and this is more his affair than mine, intellect, like other human agents, depends much on its environment. Through this environment intellect may be all light for certain 'veracities' and all darkness for others. By this environment intellect may be blinded and debased, or may be neutralised and enfeebled. There may be states of society, and an apparatus of human life, in which the myriad forms of human self regard are so developed as to bind the soul in a network which though invisible is of steel, the scales of sympathy and antipathy so weighted, as to impart a hopeless bias to character in the wrong direction, among those very classes which (as I believe) are best endowed by nature and have the largest opportunities from position, so that in extreme cases all the advantages of intellect may be nullified by darkening moral influences and those who ought to know the best and do the best may become a standing conspiracy against things the truest, the greatest and the noblest, against all the redeeming forces of our nature.

86

*Professor Tyndall to WEG, 9 March 1890*[1]
I have said many a time since that if you really knew what you were doing in Ireland—the bigotry and ignorance which your measures would establish, and the enlightenment and energy which they would quench—you would go to the scaffold sooner than persist in your present course.

**307** 10 March 1888 *Conversation with Charles Stewart Parnell*
ADD MS 44773 ff 48–50

*WEG's notes for this conversation*[2]
Memorandum for March 8. 1888.[3]
1. To keep the administration of the Coercion Act in its details before the eye of the country, and of Parliament by speeches, and by statistics.
2. To remain detached and in a condition to accept a settlement from the Tories.
3. What course should be taken if the government offer measures good in themselves, but insufficient for a settlement? Accept without prejudice?
4. Non-Irish legislation to be promoted (but dissentients will not as a body dissent from the government).
5. Does the idea of the American Union afford a practical point of departure?

*WEG's memorandum of the conversation*[4]
I made the inclosed note of points which I wished to include in my conversation with Mr. Parnell today.

He looked not ill, but far from strong. He gave a favourable account of his health.

I pressed the first point rather strongly. He did not appear to have

[1] ADD MS 44509, f 241.
[2] ADD MS 44773, f 48.
[3] The conversation took place on 10 March.
[4] ADD MS 44773, ff 49–50.

87

considered it much, but to give weight to it and he made a note on the subject.

The second I merely set out before him *pour acquit de conscience*. He said he expected nothing from the Tories as long as they should feel that they could get on without concession.

On the third point, as indeed on all, he was extremely moderate and reasonable: and I was not entirely without an apprehension that the energies of his political pursuit were somewhat abated by his physical condition.

He thought the turning point lay in a Dublin Parliament. He did not see what could be given short of this that would be worth taking: whereas if this could be had, even with insufficient powers, it might be accepted. I understood him to mean might be accepted as a beginning.

I mentioned Sir E. Watkin's idea of provincial assemblies with a contingent power of election from themselves to constitute a body which should meet in Dublin for particular purposes. He thought it conceivable that this might resolve itself into a question of the mode of election.

He quite agreed as to no. 4.

Did not think the Irish people would be impatient even if Home Rule were not mooted this year in the House of Commons.

Believed crime, properly so called, was declining.

My chief point with him was that expressed in no. 5. On this ground, that the opponents never so far as I know have condemned the American system as a possible basis of a plan of Home Rule: and I have always held the hope that it might in case of need supply at least a phrase to cover them in point of consistency. I said I was aware of no difficulty unless it should be found to lie in the incapacity to touch contracts. On the practical working of which, I had not been able to obtain sufficient information.

He thought this idea might be made a groundwork. Did not wholly repel even the idea of parliamentary intervention to stop extreme and violent proceedings in Dublin. I said a court would fix the lines of the respective provinces better than parliamentary action.

Undoubtedly as a whole his tone was very conservative.

*March 10. 1888.*

He was much pleased to know I had declared the question of money required further investigation.

**308** 18–19 December 1889 *Charles Stewart Parnell's visit to Hawarden: Liberal policy on Ireland*
ADD MS 44773 ff 170–171

*Secret.* 1890.[1]

After very long delay, of which I do not know the cause, Mr. Parnell's promised visit came off last week. He appeared well and cheerful and proposed to accompany (without a gun) my younger sons who went out shooting.

Nothing could be more satisfactory than his conversation; full as I thought of good sense from beginning to end.

I had prepared carefully all the points that I could think of,[2] or recall from any suggestions of others, as possible improvements (as to essence or as to prudential policy) in the Irish Government Bill or Land Bill.

I did not press him to positive conclusions, but learnt pretty well the leaning of his mind; and ascertained that, so far as I could judge, nothing like a crotchet, or an irrational demand, from his side, was likely to interfere with the proper freedom of our deliberations when the proper time comes for practical steps.

The points were numerous, and I propose to reserve the recital of them until we meet in London, which, if (as I assume) the judges have made their report, I think we ought to do not later than the Saturday, or perhaps the Friday, before Tuesday the 11th when the session opens.

I may say, however, that we were quite agreed in thinking the real difficulty lies in determining the particular form in which an Irish representation may have to be retained at Westminster. We conversed at large on the different modes. He has no absolute or foregone conclusion.

He emphatically agreed in the wisdom and necessity of reserving our judgment on this matter until a crisis is at hand.

Will those of my late colleagues who may see this paper kindly note the fact by their initials.            *December 23. 1889.*

S[pencer] 24.12.89
R[osebery] 27.12.89
W[illiam] V[ernon] H[arcourt] 29.12.89

---

[1] '1890' (*recte* 1889) added later.
[2] ADD MS 44773, ff 155–169.

G[ranville] memorandum forwarded 30.12.89
H[erschell] 1.1.90
K[imberley] 2.1.90
J[ohn] M[orley] 3.1.90
R[ipon] 4.1.90
J[ames] S[tansfeld] 7.1.90
A[nthony] J[ohn] M[undella] 8/1/90
H[enry] C[ampbell]-B[annerman] 20.1.90
A[rnold] M[orley] 25.1.90

**309** 30 November 1890 *Conversation with Justin McCarthy: relations
with Parnell following the O'Shea divorce case*
ADD MS 56448

Proposal of November 30.

'Will Mr. Gladstone, Sir W. Harcourt and Mr. Morley entrust Mr.
Justin McCarthy with letters promising that in the event of the return
of the Liberal party to power they will introduce a Bill under which

1. The control of the constabulary shall be given to an Irish executive
   responsible to an Irish Parliament.
2. Such Parliament shall have power to deal with the land question.
3. These shall be *vital* conditions of the Bill which is not to pass without
   them.'

This was the purport of the written proposal of Mr. McCarthy as
written down by me on Mr. McCarthy's quitting us—not a copy.

Mr. McCarthy added two assurances.

1. That this was confidential, and under no circumstances to be
   divulged.
2. That power over the land question meant only in so far as it should
   not have been disposed of by the Imperial Parliament.

My answer was, with some collateral observations, that I could deal
in relation to the Home Rule question only with the Irish parliamentary
party through its leader or those whom it authorised to approach me,
whereas Mr. Parnell had renounced this party and going from it had
assumed a right of appeal to the Irish nation. I therefore had no 'full
powers'.

Sir W. Harcourt came in half way and gave a reply arriving at the
same point.

*Docketed:* November 30. Memorandum of conversation with Mr.
McCarthy; at 2.30 p.m.

**310**  15 January 1891   *Conversation with John Morley: the Irish National-*
*ists*
ADD MS 44773 f 210

While red-hot shot is continually fired into the Nationalists and all
idea of what is termed concession to them, judgment is fast going by
default against the people of Ireland as disloyalists, robbers, enemies
to England and to the unity of the Empire.

It is the *Nationalists* with whom it lies to defend the people of Ireland
against these heavy charges.

Are they doing it? Dare they do it? *Must* they present one face to
their contributors oversea, and leave it [to] us to patch upon them
another as towards Great Britain?

Thus in substance I spoke to Morley at the close of our conversation
today.                                                         *January 15.*

**311**  *post* 9 June 1891   *WEG's reaction to the Tranby Croft case*
ADD MS 44773 ff 234–235

*The famous Tranby Croft case, tried in the Court of Queen's Bench 1–9 June
1891, was an action for slander brought by Sir William Gordon-Cumming, who
had been accused of cheating at cards during a house party at Tranby Croft,
Yorkshire. The sensational nature of the case was increased by the Prince of
Wales giving evidence for the plaintiff. The jury found for the defendants.*

Experience has convinced me that resort to games of chance in the
manner which has recently been made known by the proceedings in
the Court of Queen's Bench gives public offence, places in the way of
temptation those who may not always be able to resist it, and cannot
tend to raise the[1] tone and standard of social life.

Feeling that my own example may be quoted in connection with this
very painful incident, I am desirous to take some immediate step which
besides relieving me from the grave responsibility of being accessory
to social and moral mischief, may in itself be of public advantage.

I have therefore resolved henceforward personally to abandon all
use of games of chance, whether by cards or otherwise, which could
even by the strictest judgment of men of sense and honour be deemed
to approach to the character or give however remotely countenance
to the practice of gambling.                                   [*Undated.*]

---

[1] MS: to.

**312**  25 November 1892  *Audience with the Queen*
ADD MS 44774 ff 163–164

Topics.
 1. Inquiry for the Queen's health.
 2. The fogs of London and Windsor.
 3. The Laureateship. W. Watson.
 4. The dowager Duchess of Sutherland: the Duke's state as to money.
 5. The Roumanian marriage. The Pope's dispensation has been given. Marriage of the present King and punishment of the priest.
 6. Lord Acton: not yet personally known to the Queen.
 7. Condition of Lady Kimberley.
 8. Has Mrs. Gladstone still a nephew who is a master at Eton?
 9. Dean Wellesley and Sir A. Clayton.
 10. The Dean of Peterborough.
 11. Health of the Bishop of Rochester.
 12. Agricultural distress. (Her Majesty seemed half inclined to lay it upon 'large importations'.)
 13. Commission thereupon (not desired).

These are all or nearly all the topics of conversation introduced at the audience tonight. From them may be gathered in some degree the terms of confidence between Her Majesty and her Prime Minister. Not perhaps with perfect exactitude, as she instinctively avoids points of possible difference. But then it seems that such are now all points.

*November 25. 1892.*

**313**  21 February 1894  *WEG's resignation: notes for a conversation with Sir Henry Ponsonby*[1]
ADD MS 44776 ff 51–52

 1. It is probable that when the remaining business of the session and any matter immediately connected with it have been disposed of I may have a communication to make to Her Majesty, which it might be for Her Majesty's convenience that she should have the opportunity of reflecting on before it actually reaches her.

---

[1] There are three memoranda for this conversation, which was to prepare the Queen for WEG's resignation: ADD MS 44776, ff 50, 51–52, 53–54. The above is the fullest. See also the correspondence between WEG and Ponsonby, 24–27 February: Guedalla, ii. nos. 1460–1464.

2. I am strictly bound in honour to say nothing which if it went beyond Her Majesty could have the effect of creating doubt or speculation as to the complete responsibility and solidarity of the whole government as it stands for the purpose above mentioned, if it were to go beyond Her Majesty.

3. On the other hand I have no title in making a communication to Her Majesty to impose any condition of secrecy even if only for a time.

4. The sole motive of the following inquiry is the convenience of Her Majesty.

5. In these circumstances I ask Sir H. Ponsonby whether it would be agreeable to his duty and his judgment to receive from me an indication of the communication I refer to, and to give me the assurance that I should not in any way depart by making it from that obligation of honour which I have described.

(*WEG February 21. 1894.*)

**314** 28 February 1894 *Audience with the Queen: WEG's intended retirement*[1]
ADD MS 44776 ff 57–58

I had an audience of the Queen, for 30 or 35 minutes today: doubtless my last in our official capacity. She had much difficulty in finding topics for an adequate prolongation: but fog, rain, and the coming journey to Italy all did their duty and helped. I thought I never saw her looking better. She was at the highest point of her cheerfulness. Her manner was personally kind throughout. She asked about my wife, and about the rector; also on an occasion which arose about Harry. To me she said she was sorry *for the cause* which brought about my resignation. She did not however show any curiosity for particulars as to eyes and ears.

I asked whether the day for the journey to Italy was yet fixed. Yes the Queen said she was going *on the 13th*, and it could not be later as if it were delayed she would get into Passion Week and seemed to anticipate impediments not very intelligible to me. I had told her that according

---

[1] For the Queen's account of this audience, see *L.Q.V.*, 3rd series, ii. 365–366. For her account of the audience of 2 March, of which WEG appears to have left no record, see ibid., 367.

to present appearances the Speech Council might be on Saturday [3 March] and the prorogation Monday [5 March]. For how long she asked? Not longer than a week I apprehended. That however would be till the 12th. From hence I derived the impression, an impression only, and drawn from this part of the conversation, that she has at present no idea of any thing but a simple and limited reconstruction such as is necessarily consequent upon the retirement of a Prime Minister, and has no idea of resorting to the Tories or Opposition: further that she will not ask any advice from me as to the head; and further still that she will send for Rosebery. All this grew out of the almost casual reference by me to the day of departure for Italy. It was the only part of the conversation that had any importance.

She spoke, however, of Italy and deplored its condition: did not dissent when I ascribed it mainly to ambition. She spoke of Crispi and did not like him: of course in horror at his marital proceedings. She seemed rather surprised when I said that Cavour was older than I was. She thought the Italians very friendly to us which is true. They have however expectations from us, which are[1] without foundation. She returns to London on Monday next.

I said that, if we had the Speech Council on Saturday my definitive letter might go to her on that day.[2]

Any fear that the intelligence I had to give would be a shock to her, has been entirely dispelled. Certainly the impression on my mind is that she does not even consider it a trouble, but regards it as the immediate precursor of an arrangement more agreeable.

All this is subject to illustration and modification from the immediate future. Of modification however I do not expect much.

*February 28. 1894.*

**315**  3 March 1894   *Final audience with the Queen*
ADD MS 44776 ff 59–60

Saturday, March 3. 1894.
As I crossed the quadrangle at 10.20 on my way to St. George's Chapel, I met Sir H. Ponsonby who said he was anxious to speak to me about the future. He was much impressed with the movement among a body

---

[1] The MS appears to read 'with our'.
[2] 3 March. Guedalla, ii. no. 1466.

of Members of Parliament against having any peer for Prime Minister. I signified briefly that I did not think there should be too ready a submission to such a movement. There was not time to say a great deal and I had something serious to say, so we adjourned the conversation till half past eleven, when I should return from St. George's.

He came at that time and opened on the same lines desiring to obtain from me whatever I thought proper to say as to persons in the arrangements for the future. I replied to him that this was in my view a most serious matter. All my thoughts on it were absolutely at the command of the Queen. And I should be equally at his command, if he inquired of me from her and in her name: but that otherwise my lips must be sealed. I knew from him that he was in search of information to report to the Queen, but this was a totally different matter.

I entered however freely on the general question of the movement among a section of the House of Commons. I thought it impossible to say at the moment but I should not take for granted that it would be formidable, or regard it as *in limine* disposing of the question. Up to a certain point, I thought it a duty to strengthen the hands of our small minority and little knot of ministers in the Lords by providing these ministers with such weight as attaches to high office. I related to him, but without mentioning any names, the strong resistance which I was obliged to overcome (without any assistance, I might have added) to my giving Ripon the Colonial Office, the Chancellorship of the Duchy being proposed for him instead, to which I would not consent to bring him down. All this, or rather all that touched the main point namely the point of a peer Prime Minister he without doubt reported.[1]

The Council train came down and I joined the ministers in the drawing room. I received various messages as to the time when I was to see the Queen, and when it would be most convenient to me. I interpret this variety as showing that she was nervous. It ended in fixing the time after the Council and before luncheon. I carried in with me a box containing my letter of resignation, and, the Council being over handed it to her immediately. She asked whether she ought then to read it. I said there was nothing in the letter to require it. It repeated my former letter of notice, with the requisite additions.

I must notice what though slight supplied the only incident of any

---

[1] For Ponsonby's account of this conversation, see his letter to the Queen, 3 March: *L.Q.V.*, 3rd series, ii. 369.

interest in this, perhaps rather memorable audience, which closed a service that would reach to 53 years on September 1 when I was sworn Privy Councillor before the Queen with her swollen face and eyes *laudably* red. When I came into the room and came near to take the seat she has now for some time courteously commanded, I did think she was going to break down. I do not know how I could be mistaken, it being a matter within my poor powers of vision. But perhaps I was in error. If I was not, at any rate she rallied herself, as I thought, by a prompt effort, and remained collected and at her ease. Then came the conversation which may be called neither here nor there. Its only material feature was negative. There was not one syllable on the past: except a repetition, an emphatic repetition, of the thanks she had long ago amply rendered for what I had done, a service of no great merit, in the matter of the Duke of Coburg; which I assured her would not now escape my notice if occasion should arise.[1] There was the question of eyes and ears, of German *versus* English oculists, she believing in the German as decidedly superior. Some reference to my wife, with whom she had had an interview, and had ended it affectionately. And various nothings. No touch on the subject of the last Ponsonby conversation. Was I wrong in not tendering orally my best wishes? I was afraid that any thing said by me should have the appearance of *touting*. A departing servant has some title to offer his hopes and prayers for the future: but a servant is one who has done, or tried to do service in the past. There is in all this a great sincerity. There also seems to be some little mystery as to my own case with her. I saw no sign of embarrassment or pre-occupation. The language of Wednesday's memorandum may stand.[2]

The Empress Frederick was outside in the corridor. She bade me a most kind and warm farewell, which I had done nothing to deserve.

*March 5. 1894.*

**316** 28 February–3 March 1894 *The Queen's reception of WEG's resignation*
ADD MS 44776 ff 61–62

The Queen's note addressed to me on Saturday March 3[3] is the only

---

[1] See Guedalla, nos. 1440, 1441, 1474.
[2] For the Queen's account, see *L.Q.V.*, 3rd series, ii. 370.
[3] Guedalla, ii. no. 1467.

*pièce* proceeding from Her Majesty in the process which has wound up an account reaching over 52½ years from September 1. 1841 when I was sworn of the Privy Council.

There were also three interviews; one on Wednesday February 28: one on Friday March 2: and a very short one on Saturday March 3. They add nothing material to the contents of the brief note. On the Wednesday she expressed her regret for the '*cause*' somewhat emphasised which had brought about the intimation of a probable event then conveyed to her, and at the last on Saturday she had expressed anew, orally, thanks for my efforts in the case of the Duke of Coburg, which had already been given in writing at the time of the little debate in the House of Commons.

Substantially then the proceeding was brief though the interviews were greatly eked out with secondary matter.

The same brevity perhaps prevails in settling a tradesman's bill, when it reaches over many years.

The note says it is not written for the purpose of accepting my resignation as this had been previously done.

But the facts stand thus. There was no tender of resignation made by me until I wrote out at Windsor on Saturday forenoon the letter in which it was contained. It appeared to me to require some moderate length and particularity of statement. I put it into a box and carried this box, after the Council, into the small room where the Council meets. I gave it to the Queen and told her it contained my tender of resignation.

(It was at this point that there occurred, if at all, what would have been indeed a circumstance in my rather dry record.)

She asked me if she need read it before conversing with me. I said that rested wholly with Her Majesty. Then followed the short conversation: and on retirement I kissed hands. Not one word was said of the resignation: and it seems that if it was accepted it was in some way accepted *before* it was tendered.

I did not on retiring, proffer service as I did in writing to the Prince of Wales:[1] for what was my service worth? Not one syllable proceeded from Her Majesty either as to the future or the past. I could not go *touting*.                                                    *March 10. 1894.*

---

[1] Morley, *The Life of William Ewart Gladstone*, iii. 510.

**317** 10 and 11 March 1894   *WEG's relations with the Queen*
ADD MS 44776 ff 63–64

At the Duke of York's dinner on Wednesday the 7th, Rosebery sat by my wife and talked freely with her. Among other things he said 'He hates the Queen, doesn't he?' She defended me. But the proper defence would have to say that anyone giving countenance to this cruel imputation, ought at least to be supplied with the evidence of some act done, or some word written or spoken, which would give countenance of some kind to it.

There is and can be no such act, no such word. In writing to Rosebery on the matter of Lansdowne's honour I certainly spoke (as a milder thing than sending him the document) in censure of a letter she had sent to me. But this, if he had no other foundation to build on, was ludicrous.

Let me now make in a few words a clean breast of it.

I am as I hope loyal to the Throne.

I admire in the Queen many fine qualities which she possesses.

I certainly used [to] admire still more: and frankly I do not see that the Queen has improved in the last twenty years. (Dean Wellesley spoke to me of a change in her before I perceived it myself.) But there is plenty of room remaining for the admiration of which I speak. Further I am grateful to the Queen as I have expressed it in my letter for many kindnesses received at various periods of my service under her.

Every one knows her attitude towards Liberalism. But taking relations to me since 1844, as a whole, there is in them something of mystery, which I have not been able to fathom, and probably never shall.

I hope my duty to her and her family has never in fact, as it has never in intention, fallen short.

And I have a new cause of gratitude to Her Majesty in her having on this last occasion admitted my wife anew to a footing of confidence and freedom. She had too long, I think, been suffering on my behalf. I am delighted that this chapter is well closed.

God save the Queen.                  *March 10 and 11. 1894.*

**318** 19 March 1894   *The same*
ADD MS 44776 ff 65–66

*Secret.* Politics.

With reference to the foregoing memorandum on the attitude of the

Queen in reference to my resignation and retirement I do think there has been some mystery about the extreme dryness of the relations which she has maintained with me now through a considerable tract of years: in contrast with those which subsisted when (in and after) in 1868 I had come in to disestablish the Irish Church.

But I think the facts of the recent juncture have been perfectly plain. On Tuesday the 28th,[1] I heard that the Queen after the drawing room was overdone, rheumatic, and out of sorts. I was quite sorry to think on Wednesday of burdening her with an interview and before it I said to Ponsonby with some feeling, 'How is the Queen today?' He answered briskly, 'Quite well'. It seems that she had conceived no idea of my resignation and personal retirement. When she found this distinctly stated to her as an immediate likelihood, the intimation acted as a sovereign remedy. She was free, cheerful, and disengaged, during the interview of that day, in an unusual degree. And so she continued to be at Windsor during the remaining interviews of the 2nd and 3rd of March. There was an evident sense of liberation, of a weight taken off her mind. Of course I do not include the moment when I seemed, rightly or wrongly, to observe a passing sign of emotion. Upon the whole it is painful to be troublesome to any one, especially to a woman, especially among women to a Queen, and to an old and much respected Queen. I am very sorry for it: and I should be much more sorry still, had I cause to suspect that I had either by wilfulness or by neglect myself caused aggravations of the mischief.          (*March 19. 1894.*)

**319**  20 March 1894   *WEG as the Sicilian mule*
ADD MS 44776 ff 67–68

*Secret*. Politics.
The force of a resemblance really compels me to put a word on paper which I had not intended, which will stand alone, and which will never pass the door of my lips on its passage to the ear of any human being.

In the autumn of 1838 I made the *giro* of Sicily from Palermo by Girgenti and Syracuse to Messina, in two or three weeks riding, on the back of a mule. The beast was wholly inaccessible to notes of kindness by voice or hand, and was disposed to lag, so that our muleteer,

[1] *recte* 27th.

Michele, used to call out, '*Pugna, signor, pugna*': an uncertain [?] process of only momentary effect. But we rode usually with little interval from 5 a.m. to 4 p.m. and its undemonstrative, unsympathetic service was not inefficiently performed. In due time we arrived at Messina to take our departure from the island. There my mule and I of necessity parted company.

But I well remember having at the time a mental experience, which was not wholly unlike a sense of indigestion. I had been on [the] back of the beast for many scores of hours; it had done me no wrong: it had rendered me much valuable service. Yet it was in vain to argue. There was the fact staring me in the face, I could not get up the smallest shred of feeling for the brute, I could neither love nor like it.

A rule of three sum is all that is necessary to conclude with. What that Sicilian mule was to me, I have been to the Queen; and the fortnight or three weeks are represented by 52 or 53 years. A friend, now a peer, told me he knew shameful things had been reported of me to her: and from one point of view I have been pleased. I recollect that in consequence of less grave rumours which had reached her in 1868 about Clarendon she sent me a message before the ministerial crisis to express her desire that he should not be Foreign Secretary in the forthcoming administration; a dictum of much rashness from which she ingenuously receded.                                      *March 20. 1894.*

**320**  21 March 1894  *Conversation with Edward Nettleship, the ophthalmic surgeon*
ADD MS 44790 ff 105–106

Memorandum.
I spent nearly an hour today with Mr. Nettleship who spoke with great clearness and frankness and like a man who knew what he was about. He examined my eyes by strong lights very minutely, and we conversed on a number of points relating to them.

The upshot was simple and in some respects went beyond my expectation. Especially in this, that it is not now thought necessary to wait for maturity of cataract in a second eye before operating on the first. He considers, as I understood him that the cataract in my right eye is ripe and that an operation might at once or almost at once take place;

but he recommended for the greatest advantage that it should be postponed until the longer days. He would like a time not earlier than May
nor later than October. I told him that for my general purposes the
sooner it could be the better.

There is hardly any pain; not always though usually consciousness
that the operation is going on. I asked what precautions were usually
taken against motion of the head or face which might disturb the
process. He said this was mainly confined to excitable cases and appeared to think there was no danger in a case like mine. I had told him
I could formerly resist pain but that I did not now feel very certain of
myself as against some twitch, or sudden movement, without the
power of bringing forethought to bear upon it. I asked if the head were
held by others to prevent movement. Not commonly I understood: but
there is no difficulty whatever in having it done.

I forgot to ask about the method to be pursued, and the probable
time of confinement, after the operation.

Cocaine is used to make the eyeballs insensible.

He does not object to the use of *bella donna* during the intermediate
period to improve vision temporarily.

He attaches great importance to good general health: and he also
desires the absence of all marked gouty tendency. I showed him my
chief gouty indications on the middle finger of the left hand. He seemed
to attach no sort of importance to them.

Almost before I was out of the house, the Press Association was down
on him for a report but he declined to give any without my permission.
*I* advised in reply saying no more than that there was no circumstance
of complication.

On the whole the result of the interview was every way satisfactory
to me and a cause for thankfulness.

*10 Downing Street. March 21. 1894.*

**321**  29 June 1894  *The Eton Debating Society*
ADD MS 44776 ff 81–84

June 29. Memorandum Lady Lyell's conversation (correct?).

Lady Lyell, wife of the Liberal M.P. for Orkney, whose son is in the
sixth form at Eton and I believe a distinguished boy, was here yesterday
and told me as follows.

There are now as it appears two societies among the elder members
of the school—one called Pop and the other the Literary Society.

She visited the premises of Pop, and found the room abundantly supplied with sporting magazines and papers. There were in it two pictures, one of Ladas, the other of his jockey.

I understand from her that except in connection with the subjects just indicated Pop has no activity or function—being a club of no very elevated order.

But—and here it was that she raised my astonishment to a high point—this club, thus equipped, is materially and bodily by regular succession the representative of the primitive Eton debating society, founded in 1811, the mother and model I believe of all the debating societies of the schools and universities of the kingdom.

In my time this society rose (not through my agency) to a condition of prosperous activity: it numbered on its lists all the most distinguished boys—I will name only Arthur Hallam, the subject of *In Memoriam*.

Such had been its character from the days of its formation. Lord Derby, Lord Morpeth, Lord Taunton, Mr. Praed, were among its active members.

It fostered no small portion of the intellectual life of the school: and its proceedings were conducted, though under *jealous* limitations imposed by the authorities, yet with considerable spirit.

In my time it had another and a really rare and curious characteristic. Its records were kept (perhaps for a couple of years) with devoted care and *consummate knowledge* (mainly) by Milnes Gaskell. They still exist, and are consulted, and constitute in my opinion [a record] of rare interest and value.

The honour awarded them seems to be that belonging by succession to Pop they rub shoulders with its sporting magazines and periodicals.

I own I should have supposed that some motive—possibly decency—might have led to their being transferred to the Literary Society. I confidently [hope] that they are only withheld from it through the operation of some temporary accident. That they are considered by the ruling powers of Pop as its legitimate property I will not for a moment believe.

How the transformation of the society was brought about, I do not fully know: but I believe it began with the admission to the old Eton Society, in honour and goodwill, of the captain of the eleven and the boats.

See Miss Hannah More's *Peter Parley the Porter*.          *June 29. 1894.*

# APPENDIX 1

**Gladstone on the Conservative Party**

ADD MSS 44766 f 117, 44769 f 35, 44770 f 4, 44773 f 195, 44792 f 196

Politics.

Causes tending to help the Conservative party and give it at least an occasional preponderance though a minority of the nation.

1. Greater wealth available for the expences of elections.
2. Greater unity from the comparative scantiness of such explosive matter within the party, as is supplied by the activity of thought and opinion in the Liberal party, not always sufficiently balanced: with which activity self-seeking is apt to mix.
3. The existence of powerful professional classes more or less sustained by privilege or by artfully constructed [?] monopoly: the army, the law, the clergy.
4. The powerful influence attached to the possession of land, and its distribution in few hands not merely from legal arrangements but from economic causes.
5. The impossibility of keeping the *public* mind always lively and intent upon great national interests, while the opposite sentiment of class never slumbers.
6. The concentration of the higher social influences, thus associated with Toryism, at the fixed seat of government, and their ready and immediate influence from day to day on the action of the legislature through the different forms of social organisation used by the wealthy and leisured class. *August 14. 1882.*[1]

Suggestion for Hamilton (to Ponsonby) in explanation of my letter of February 27–8. 1885.[2]

Conservatism so-called, in its daily practice, now depends largely on inflaming public passion, and thereby has lost the main element which made it really Conservative, and qualified it to resist excessive and dangerous innovation. This is my conviction, but no doubt it would be ascribed by many to my prejudice and partiality. *February 28. 1885.*[3]

---

[1] ADD MS 44766, f 117.
[2] See Hamilton, ii. 804.
[3] ADD MS 44769, f 35.

Toryism in other days had two legs to stand upon: a sound leg, and a lame leg. Its sound leg was reverence: its lame leg was class interest. Reverence it has almost forgotten. It no longer leans upon that leg. It leans now upon its lame leg, the leg of class interest, more much more; and to mend the matter, as it stumps along, it calls out progress.

Does Lady Herbert remember the *only* bitter and contemptuous thing, that Sidney Herbert ever said in Parliament? and what, and who, drew it from him?[1]                              *December 10. 1885.*[2]

In my youth, the quality and habit of reverence made men Conservatives.

So far as I see there is no such tendency, no such association, now.

Reverence is not in fashion on either side of politics. It is largely at a discount with both. But the offence of forgetting it is very different, and much aggravated in the Conservative: just as a Liberal would be the more guilty when caught out in an indifference to liberty.

These two are I think the great poles on which a sound creed revolves and is secure.[3]

I was trained in a Conservative school of (not the modern: even the name is changed)
1. Economy.
2. Peace.
3. Sound and strict finance.
4. Anti-jobbing.
5. Maintenance of the sound traditions of Parliament.
                                        of administration.[4]

---

[1] There is nothing relevant to this document in WEG's correspondence with Lady Herbert (ADD MS 44212).

[2] ADD MS 44770, f 4.

[3] ADD MS 44773, f 195. Undated.

[4] ADD MS 44792, f 196. Undated.

# APPENDIX 2

**E. W. Hamilton's account of the formation of WEG's third ministry, 29 January–6 February 1886**

ADD MS 48642 ff 113–136[1]

*Friday, 29 January.* (Mentmore). Lord Salisbury returned from Osborne early today; but when I left town (six o'clock) Mr. G. had received no summons as yet. I heard from Sir H. Ponsonby this morning. His views on the situation accorded with mine; and he is advising the Queen to send for Mr. G. at once.

The latest rumour this afternoon was that Goschen had been sent for to advise.

Went again this morning to see Lord Wolverton whom Mr. G. likes to have by him on these occasions. According to him, Mr. G. is beginning to face the difficulty about Lord Granville—a most painful effort to him. How is Lord Granville to be approached? Who could be commissioned to open the subject with him? I say, Lord Spencer.

I went on to Carlton House Terrace. All hope of Hartington is at an end; but he has parted company with Mr. G. as the best of friends. Mr. G. was much pleased and even touched by Hartington's behaviour. Notwithstanding Hartington's great loss, Herbert Gladstone who inherits his father's sanguine temperament was in good spirits.

The composition of the Cabinet will be a most difficult task, what with the awkwardness of dealing with the foreign secretaryship, Dilke's temporary disability, the mood of Chamberlain and Harcourt, and the doubtful attitude of others besides Hartington. Rosebery was to be Foreign Secretary. The only question is—will he face the great responsibility of the office? I cannot see any man fitted for the Chancellorship of the Exchequer. Childers cannot go back. Chamberlain would be a strong man and a short experience at the Exchequer would probably knock out of his head all the 'ransom' nonsense and all his heterodox financial doctrines; but would not his appointment produce a perfect scare among the propertied classes?

Later in the morning R. Grosvenor came over to me from Mr. G. who wanted to know what amount of credence ought to be attached to the supposition that the Queen will, if she sends for him, insist on a

---

[1] From the diary of E. W. Hamilton.

dissolution or the setting aside of his Irish policy. I could only say that I thought it natural and therefore probable.[1] R. Grosvenor (whose loss to Mr. G. will be very great) thinks Mr. G. will be content to form a government on a basis which is practically limited to an inquiry into the feasibility and safety of a legislative body for Ireland. This will be rather a climb down. One of my fears is that he will break down in the process of constructing a measure.

I cannot keep my fingers out of the political pie. They itch to rejoin the political fray; and I would give much to return to Downing Street. But I feel obliged to dismiss the idea of this. I have no business to leave in commission a place of so much responsibility and work. Moreover I could not ask that I might be temporarily replaced by one of those over whose heads I was put; and put by the Tories.

I tried this evening to make up a Cabinet; but the elements of its composition are too uncertain to admit of this. It looks as if we shall run rather short of material; but all depends on the number of his late colleagues who will rejoin Mr. G.

*Saturday, 30 January.* We learnt this morning at Mentmore that Sir H. Ponsonby made a midnight communication to Mr. G. last night to the effect that he was to try his hand at forming a government.[2]

I received a summons while out shooting to go to Mr. G.; and I put myself into the earliest train. On arrival in town I went at once to Carlton House Terrace. Mr. G. was quite satisfied with the message conveyed to him by Ponsonby. There were hardly any conditions

---

[1] See Hamilton's memorandum for Ponsonby, 27 January, summarised on ff 107–111. Hamilton writes about the Queen's sending for WEG: 'But it is hardly possible that the Queen, after her recent solemn declaration that she will not allow the fundamental law of the Irish Union to be touched, will not impose conditions. She may reasonably urge that if he becomes her first minister, he must either give up or postpone organic change of the constitution, or advise a dissolution, in order that, before so great a constitutional change is taken in hand, he must have a mandate from the country.' After discussing the various alternatives, he suggests Rosebery should be sent for. 'I own that my personal leanings are against the resumption of office by Mr. G. I cannot bear the thought of his being at his age over weighted with the tremendous cares and difficulties which would beset him not only at home but abroad; and the imposition of conditions by the Queen—reasonable and constitutional conditions—would give him a plausible loophole for escape.'

[2] Ponsonby to the Queen, 30 January, *L.Q.V.*, 3rd series, i. 27–28.

attached by the Queen, except that Lord Granville was not to return to the Foreign Office and that Dilke was not to be admitted into the Cabinet. Mr. G.'s great difficulty at starting will be Lord Granville. It is thought that he will only join if he is put back again at the Foreign Office. It will be a horribly painful business to Mr. G. He cannot possibly get on without Lord Granville as a colleague; and it will go horribly against Mr. G.'s grain to hint at Lord Granville's removal. Mr. G. had seen Chamberlain who will join subject to certain conditions. Mr. G. has practically fixed upon Arnold Morley as whip; and as A. Morley is now out of court for private secretary Mr. G. has placed the composition of his secretariat in my hands. I shall plump for Henry Primrose. I am afraid there will be too many of the old lot in the Cabinet: Mr. G. is too tender hearted. I am also afraid there is no chance of getting Henry James: he committed himself too deeply to his constituents. He is torn between loyalty to those pledges and loyalty to Mr. G. I saw him this afternoon: and I confess I do not see how he could enter the government except at a great loss of self-respect. I met him outside Brooks's. He asked me to come into the club with him and have a little talk. He produced out of his pocket a cutting containing a report of a speech he had made to his constituents to the effect that not for twenty Mr. Gladstones would he consent to grant Home Rule to Ireland. 'Do you think', he said, 'I can join Mr. G.'s government in view of that speech? You know how I revere Mr. G. and how great is the effort I would make for him. Can I in order to avoid deserting him explain away what I said by calling a special meeting of my constituents?' It was I said a matter entirely that he must settle with his own conscience; but I confessed I should be very sorry to have to do the job myself.

I dined at Chamberlain's, sitting between Sir W. Harcourt and Froude. Sir W. Harcourt was, I found, very sore and in one of his worst humours. He saw everybody going to Carlton House Terrace except himself. He was slighted, because Mr. G. felt sure of his co-operation; and Mr. G. would never put himself out for his friends. All this is bad form and an unnecessary explosion. He will however no doubt join, though he has no belief in the efficacy of Mr. G.'s recipe and declares he would prefer standing out. If he joined, he might (he said) have one satisfaction—he might have another chance of hearing Childers make up his mind in the Cabinet which he (Childers) was always going to do, but never could do.

I had a talk with Chamberlain after dinner. He joins but reserves to himself complete freedom of action when Mr. G.'s Irish scheme is matured. Chamberlain, at present minded, has no belief in it. He doubts whether it is feasible; he is certain that the guarantees which Mr. G. will require will not be forthcoming. Nor does he think it necessary to go as far as Mr. G. intends to go. He (Chamberlain) is convinced that the Irishmen might now be taken on the hop: they would not dare to refuse a broad settlement of the land question coupled with local government bodies or provincial councils—his own pet scheme, towards which he naturally still turns a fond parental eye. So Chamberlain's innings might be a short and merry one; and I am not sure that Mr. G. does right to take him in on such conditions.

There were several new M.P.s at dinner—young Lawson (*Daily Telegraph* fils) among the number, who is said to be a promising young fellow. Buckle (*Times*) was also there. He continues to make a dead set against Mr. G. and his policy; and pins his faith to the left centre, Hartington and company.

The general belief is that the new government will not last many weeks. Altogether, I am low in my mind. But Mr. G. is Hobson's choice; and the real hope is that Mr. G., as has often happened before, will prove himself in the right and be found to have more foresight than most of us.

*Sunday, 31 January.* A very exciting, interesting, and bustling day, which I began by firing off a letter to Carlton Terrace to represent Harcourt's soreness and Chamberlain's half-heartedness.

I followed this up by going there later in the morning. I found the difficulty about Lord Granville as great as ever. Mr. G. told me he was perfectly ready to disregard the dead set made against Lord Granville by the press and the party; that he would make any arrangement which was agreeable to Lord Granville—he would gladly give up the Premiership and serve under Lord Granville in any capacity he liked; but that he could not sacrifice public interests to private feelings. He could not put back Lord Granville at the Foreign Office because he had un-doubted proof that Lord Granville had in the latter days of the late government showed signs of not being up to so heavy an administrative post. This was no reflection on Lord Granville because there was no instance this century of the assumption of the Foreign Secretaryship by a man over seventy. Lord Granville, looking very haggard and troubled came in after luncheon. Each apparently thought the other would broach the disagreeable subject; but neither could summon up courage to allude to it. So no way was made. Lord Spencer had broken the ground with Lord Granville without avail. As I was dining with Mr. Leveson Gower, I was commissioned to use Mr. G.'s new arguments about age as well as physical infirmity, and to try to get the brother to make a further representation. I executed my commission. After some hesitation, Mr. Leveson consented to go and see his brother again. He was then to come over and report to Mr. G. We waited anxiously till a late hour when, instead of Mr. Leveson's appearing, there came a letter from Lord Granville[1] written in charming terms but containing a refusal to join unless he returned to the Foreign Office. His appointment to any other office (so he contended) would weaken his hands in the task, already difficult enough, of leading the House of Lords. It would be a declaration of failure. He must therefore stand aside, feeling sure that he could render greater assistance to Mr. G. in an independent position than in a degraded official capacity. Poor Mr. G. was in despair; and he determined to make another appeal to Lord Granville, suggesting that Lord Granville should spontaneously resign his claim to the Foreign Office and declaring that any and every other office was at his disposal.[2] I was sent across the road with this letter. I don't think I ever felt in a much more awkward and difficult position. I sent it up to him; and it was some time before he came down—he was presumably consulting Lady Granville. At last he appeared, very haggard and evidently in a very perplexed state of mind. After a few common-place remarks, I mustered up my courage to say that Mr. G. was very anxious for an answer, in view of his having to start early for Osborne the next morning. Could he entrust me with a message? After remaining silent for a second or two which seemed to be many minutes, he said he would sleep over the matter. So back I went to Mr. G. empty-handed.

With this uncertainty about Lord Granville, Mr. G. has been able to make but small progress with the disposal of places. He has confined himself to filling up one or two (what he terms) 'special' appointments —to wit the Lord Chancellorship with F. Herschell, the War Office with Childers, the Admiralty with Chamberlain and the Irish Secretary-ship with J. Morley. I was sent up in the afternoon to try and smooth over Sir W. Harcourt, and to prepare him for Mr. G.'s calling at tea time. In the course of conversation I told Sir W. Harcourt I did not see

---

[1] Ramm (1883–1886), no. 1763.
[2] Ibid., no. 1764.

how Mr. G. could take Chamberlain on conditions which might involve his breaking away a week or two hence. Harcourt said: 'But we are all in the same boat. We none of us believe in Mr. G.'s plan; but we have no alternative policy to suggest. It is just as if Mr. G. had declared that he had a scheme for moving traffic by balloons. Some of us, like Harting-ton and H. James don't believe, and have publicly declared their dis-belief in balloons. Those have to stand aside altogether. Others like Chamberlain and myself recognise the existence of balloons; and though we do not believe that they can be turned to account as a motive power, we feel bound to approach the consideration of Mr. G.'s boasted inven-tion and to see if it can be worked out practically. If the invention prove, as we expect, to be unworkable or unsafe, we must then give it up and take our own line.' I did not tell Sir W. Harcourt that the Lord Chan-cellorship was filled up, which, as I discovered later, Mr. G. intended me to do; and Mr. G. avoided the subject when he called, confining himself to an offer of high office, not particularised. Consequently in the evening Sir W. Harcourt followed up Mr. G.'s visit with a lengthy document[1] making several stipulations, raising fresh difficulties, and hinting that he wished to be heard as to the disposal of places. As he appeared still to have his eye fixed on the Woolsack, Mr. G. took the bull by the horns and disabused him of this idea by announcing Herschell's appointment.

These personal difficulties try Mr. G. more than anything else; and when I left him tonight he was much bowed down; but he still maintains his pluck which is certainly an extraordinary characteristic of his. Thus far the process of hatching a Cabinet has been one of true labour.

*Monday, 1 February.* Went round early to see Sir W. Harcourt again. I found him in bed, more reasonable and more complaisant, though, alluding to Mr. G.'s visit yesterday at which the Lord Chancellorship was not mentioned, he complained that Mr. G. was not straight enough with his colleagues. Mr. G.'s letter however had had the desirable effect, and Sir W. Harcourt was ready to submit and even to return to the detested Home Office. I telegraphed this at once to Mr. G. who went down to Osborne this morning—a long day for a man in his 77th year. However he seemed none the worse for it this evening, when I had a long talk with him. He was in his most charming of humours and in good spirits. What had really cheered him was Lord Granville's change

---

[1] ADD MS 44200, ff 15–18.

of mood. After sleeping over Mr. G.'s final appeal, Lord Granville determined to defer to Mr. G.'s strongly expressed wishes, and he is now prepared to enter the Cabinet. The Colonies is the appointment for which he seems most inclined; and so of course he will have it; but it would have been infinitely better in the interests of the public and likewise in his own interests had he elected the Presidency of the Council which would have been a dignified refuge for him. To go from one administrative post to another is to accentuate his failure at the office which he relinquishes. He has certainly behaved with extraordinary loyalty and shewn that he possesses the most charming of dispositions. He even has hinted at Rosebery's appointment to the Foreign Office. But to return to Mr. G.'s conversation tonight. He was quite satisfied with his audience at Osborne; and talked much of the materials with which to form his Cabinet. He was very outspoken about Chamberlain. Chamberlain was wanting in straightforwardness. He was not to be trusted. He sadly lacked public spirit. Contrast Chamberlain with a man like Henry James. Mr. G. expatiated on the merits of James. 'That is indeed a splendid fellow and I do not see how I am to get on without him to help me in the House of Commons.' He subsequently broached the subject of his Irish scheme, touching on his ideas for meeting the financial difficulty. He seems minded to require Ireland to pay a fixed contribution towards imperial expenditure—probably one twelfth in order to let her down easy—though I do not see how this would work. Supposing a national emergency arose and a great addition had to be made to imperial charges, is Ireland not to be required to contribute towards that addition?

The personal difficulties are not decreasing. Childers, whom Mr. G. proposes to bring back to the War Office (it was quite unnecessary to bring him back at all) is strongly objected to in the highest circles; and Chamberlain cries off the Admiralty. I understand the prospect of an official residence, and of having to entertain, rather deters Chamberlain from that post. The place he would have liked is the Chancellorship of the Exchequer; and being unable to get it himself he is already beginning to stipulate that he will not stand there being placed over his head in that place any one of less official standing than himself. He certainly is unlike a man such as Henry James with whom I was dining tonight. Had he joined he would have had a right to claim the Lord Chancellorship. Instead of asserting that claim he admitted his own unfitness for the post. He had 'served two masters' too much—politics and law; and consequently did not feel equal to occupy a post which entailed the review of all judicial decisions.

*Tuesday, 2 February.* Mary Gladstone was married this morning at St. Margaret's to Drew. Marriage making did not conveniently combine with Cabinet making; but in church Mr. G. looked as if he had nothing in the world to do but to give away a daughter. She looked remarkably well—quietly but very nicely dressed; six pretty little girls in simple white attire attended her as bridesmaids. There was a great crowd inside and outside the church; and the Prince and Princess swelled the throng. Everything went off admirably.

After securing the dispatch at the Colonial Office of a telegram to Gibraltar to ask, by Mr. G.'s desire, the opinion of Sir J. Adye about Childers as an administrator, and after a short spell at the Treasury, I joined the wedding party at Carlton House Terrace. At the door I met Rosebery who had just been offered the Foreign Office. At any rate one of the appointments on which I had set my heart has been made; and though very high expectations have been formed of him, I have sufficient confidence in him to believe that those expectations will be fully realised.

The Cabinet has made considerable progress today. Sir W. Harcourt is to go to the Chancellorship of the Exchequer, Chamberlain to the Local Government Board,[1] Campbell Bannerman probably to the War Office where he will be highly welcomed. Sir W. Harcourt's appointment is the one which will take most people by surprise, and no wonder, considering how he has always denounced the Treasury as the incarnation of obstruction. It a little shocks the Treasury mind; but personally I am glad. I have always got on with him; and he has always been very kind to me. I have told him we shall all do our best to prove to him that the Treasury is not quite the useless institution which he has made it out to be. I am glad that Mr. G. has not pressed Childers for the War Office, considering how *ingrata* a *persona* he is to the Royal Family.

The Prince of Wales being anxious to know how the Cabinet was progressing, I went with Mr. G.'s leave to Marlborough House before dinner to report the progress. He evinced great interest in the construction of the government and expressed himself well satisfied with such appointments as I was permitted to make known to him. He

---

[1] 'Board of Trade' deleted.

talked for some time about men and places, and most sensibly. It was a great relief to him to know that Childers is not to be forced upon the Queen as her War Secretary.

I learn from Sir H. Ponsonby that the main reason of the Queen's delay about sending for Mr. G. was hesitation due to his repeated declarations that he intended to give up public life—not an unnatural assumption. When Sir H. Ponsonby saw Mr. G. late on Friday he admitted the reason of the Queen but said that matters having so changed of late he could not remain a passive spectator if his services were required by the Queen.

Mr. G. thanked me tonight for what I had done—little enough it has really been.

*Wednesday, 3 February.* The Cabinet is made. The offices have been finally disposed of in this way.

| | |
|---|---|
| First Lord of the Treasury | Mr. Gladstone |
| Lord Chancellor | Sir F. Herschell |
| Lord President of the Council | Lord Spencer |
| Home Secretary | Mr. Childers |
| Foreign Secretary | Lord Rosebery |
| Colonial Secretary | Lord Granville |
| Indian Secretary | Lord Kimberley |
| War Secretary | Mr. Campbell Bannerman |
| Chancellor of the Exchequer | Sir W. Harcourt |
| First Lord of the Admiralty | Lord Ripon |
| President of the Local Government Board | Mr. Chamberlain |
| President of the Board of Trade | Mr. Mundella |
| Secretary for Scotland | Mr. Trevelyan |
| Chief Secretary for Ireland | Mr. John Morley |

Fourteen in all: eight commoners and six peers. Round men have had to be put in square places—the inevitable result of personal difficulties. Mr. G. having committed himself to Childers for the War Office had, when that office was denied to him, to find Childers another secretaryship of state. The Home Office was the only eligible one. Lord Granville's choice of the Colonies added to the complications. If he had taken the Presidency of the Council, the Colonies might have been open to Lord Ripon, and the Admiralty to Lord Spencer—the place for which Lord Spencer had a predilection. But Lord Ripon being a

Roman Catholic could not become Lord President; so the Admiralty had to be allotted to him; and Lord Spencer, who had almost first claim to choice of places but as usual was ready to defer to the convenience of others, had to return to the Lord Presidency instead of taking an administrative place. Had anybody but Harcourt been put at the Exchequer, the resentment of Chamberlain, already bad humoured enough, would have had to be incurred. Lord Northbrook declined to join. The Cabinet is fairly strong; and the only three men who could not or would not be included and who are real losses are Hartington, Goschen, and Dilke (who is still under his moral cloud). The really difficult place still to fill up is the Lord Lieutenancy; and whatever may be done with the office eventually it must be filled up in order that the Chief Secretary may be appointed. I can think of no one, unless it be Lorne; and there would probably be difficulties about him—royal and financial.

Sir H. Ponsonby whom I saw this morning said that Her Majesty had been greatly disturbed in her mind after Lord Salisbury had left her and until Mr. G. arrived; but that after she had seen Mr. G. she calmed down wonderfully. He listened so deferentially to all she had to say, and, as generally happens when they are brought together, the meeting was most harmonious. They were in short *deux coeurs* again. But this will probably be followed up by a written explosion.

Sir W. Harcourt is pleased at the prospect of assuming the Chancellorship of the Exchequer. He has taken my little dig at him in the best of humours. He says he answers to Bentinck's dictum:[1] 'When I swore to die a bachelor, I never thought to be a married man.' He declares that, like women when married, he forgets all he ever said when he was single (at the Home Office). He will 'out-Treasury the Treasury' and will leave behind him at the Treasury the reputation of being the greatest skin-flint ever known. He already regards Lingen as a profligate spendthrift.

I went again to Marlborough House this afternoon. The Prince of Wales had already written me a note, making a suggestion or two with respect to household appointments. The further progress with the Cabinet which I had to report pleased him. He has by the way given me a letter from C. Carrington to read. The new governor writes 'in

---

[1] Should be Benedick. See *Much Ado About Nothing*, Act II, Scene iii: 'When I said I would die a bachelor, I did not think I should live till I were married.'

the seventh heaven'—delighted with his reception and everything which surrounds him. It is not rash to prophesy for him the most popular of all colonial reigns. He hopes that during it the Prince and Princess may find their way out to Australia: it would be a popular coup.[1]

*Thursday, 4 February.* These latter days have certainly been among the most interesting, if not *the* most interesting, days which I have ever spent. It is impossible to record a tithe of the incidents.

Went to pay Sir W. Harcourt a visit this morning and to promise him from oneself a welcome at the Treasury. He relinquishes all claim to the Chancellor of the Exchequer's house; so Mr. G. will be able to return to Downing Street *in statu quo ante*, which will be a great convenience. I have got to find Sir W. Harcourt a good secretary.

Rosebery's appointment is the one which is by far most generally approved. It lights up what would otherwise be a dullish Cabinet.

Today is being devoted to the filling up of the smaller places. There is a terrible dearth of good men for them. The nakedness of the political land is being exposed. The party however will be well-whipped. It is a capital team—one's original selection—Arnold Morley being *prima auriga* and his assistants, E. Marjoribanks, Cyril Flower and George Leveson, whom I am very glad to see with his first step on the political ladder, and who ought to climb up it well. A place of some position, like the Postmaster-Generalship, must be found for Wolverton. Fidelity and zeal entitle him to this. Herbert Gladstone likewise must be given a tidy post. I suggest the Financial Secretaryship at the War Office. Nobody can raise a clamour at his becoming Harry Northcote's successor.

*Saturday, 6 February.* Went yesterday afternoon to take leave of Sir M. Hicks Beach. It was supposed when he came to the Treasury that he would not be the pleasantest of men to get on with. But it was an entirely erroneous supposition. He leaves behind him an extremely favourable impression with all financial officers. He exhibited much capacity for the Exchequer; and I expect he would have made his mark there, had his tenure been longer. He referred very kindly to the satisfaction with which he had regarded my appointment.

Rosebery's appointment has been received abroad with an unanimous and most remarkable chorus of approval; though such a chorus

---

[1] A sentence about Hamilton's mother's health omitted.

does not surprise one; but it is very gratifying and pleasant. I have no doubt myself that he will fulfil the expectations which, great as they are, have been formed about him.

Mr. G.'s address to his constituents appeared yesterday. It was studiously vague. It committed him to nothing and left everything open to him—a characteristic document which puzzled his colleagues—but I do not see how he could at this moment have made any declaration of policy in stronger black and white.

The difficulty about the Lord Lieutenancy of Ireland has been got over by securing Aberdeen.[1] There was hardly any choice—Lord Wolverton was one of the chosen few thought of; Lorne was not to be secured. A Scotch Presbyterian peer would have been resented in ordinary times; but at the present moment and with so strong a man as John Morley for Chief Secretary the appointment will probably pass unchallenged. Sir L. Playfair is made Vice-President of the Council— an excellent selection; Wolverton does get the Postmaster-Generalship; H. Fowler comes to the Treasury as Financial Secretary (a strong man I expect); Morley (Lord) whose scruples have been surmounted goes to the Works; Lord Kenmare resumes the office of Lord Chamberlain; Heneage after some hesitation takes the Chancellorship of the Duchy; C. Russell and H. Davey are the law officers. Most of one's friends and nominees have been run into places; but there is no superfluity of administrative or debating strength. It is impossible to say whether and how long such a government will last. It all depends on Mr. G. and his dexterity; how his plans develop themselves. The party seems to be becoming more educated up to his Irish standard; but there is a deal yet to be digested. The 'repeal of the Union' *eo nomine*, which the establishment of a legislative body in Dublin practically entails, still sticks in people's throats. This corollary of Mr. G.'s policy is unfortunate in name and even misleading; for 'repeal of the Union' sounds almost like the equivalent of separation, which it is not. Indeed the object which Mr. G. has in view is exactly the reverse: he seeks to render the countries better united: to establish a new union—a federal union. The juncture is certainly a critical one in Ireland's history. I regard it as her last chance for many a year to come. If she does not take advantage of

[1] Note by Hamilton: 'I omitted to note at time that Shaw Lefevre who was not in Parliament at the moment kindly volunteered his services to go to Ireland as a working Lord Lieutenant—an useful, not ornamental, one.'

it or abuses it, the stick must and will be substituted for the olive branch. One of the most difficult and delicate matters ahead, to which Mr. G. was referring today, is whether and how to open communication with Parnell. I think he ought to be treated with, to be treated with direct, above board, and in broad daylight; there must be no O'Shea communications and secret treaties.

I am glad to find from Mrs. G. that he is taking to his new *personnel*. Both A. Morley and Henry Primrose are getting capitally into his ways and thoroughly suiting him. I find, as I expected, that, since Mr. G. was at Osborne and though he explained himself thoroughly to the Queen, she has written him a letter of jobation[1]—a genuine blow-off of steam—very natural, and which he treated in his most conciliatory manner.

The outgoing ministers went down this morning early to surrender their seals of office; and two hours later the incoming ministers (without Mr. G.) followed in order to take over the surrendered seals. So the third administration of Mr. Gladstone is *de facto* formed.

---

[1] Probably the letter of 4 February: *L.Q.V.*, 3rd series, i. 42–43.

# APPENDIX 3

## The Gladstone Papers 1822-1977[1]
### By R. J. OLNEY

The introduction to the first volume of this edition of Gladstone's autobiographical writings drew attention to the immense mass of papers left by him at his death.[2] Although the autobiographical writings are of conspicuous importance for the light they throw on the man and his period, in quantity they form only a small fraction of his surviving archive. In this concluding volume it might accordingly seem appropriate to replace them in the context of the history of his papers as a whole.

From his Eton years until his death over seventy years later Gladstone was an indefatigable record-maker and record-keeper, both in public and in private life. His surviving journals and accounts begin in the mid 1820s, and he did not cease work on his projected autobiography until November 1897, six months before he died.[3] He wrote fluently, though in a hand which can cause problems for the uninitiated. He preferred to make fair copies in his own hand, reducing his dependence on secretaries to a minimum, and he was meticulous in dating documents. Less helpfully for the archivist, from the 1840s onwards he eschewed the bound volume for entering notes and memoranda, preferring to use loose sheets that could be re-ordered '*ad libitum*'.[4] The sheets were of sizes differing according to the type of document, the smallest being for his literary work.

Like other statesmen of the period, he spent much time at his desk writing letters on public and political matters, most of them replies to letters just received. The more important replies were mostly copied into letter-books, but letters of exceptional importance or urgency were

---

[1] During the preparation of this appendix help was most kindly given by staff of the British Library Department of Manuscripts, Lambeth Palace Library and Clwyd Record Office.

[2] *W. E. Gladstone I: Autobiographica*, 1971, 1-2.

[3] Already, by July 1894, his eyesight had deteriorated to the extent that he could not read over what he had written (Gladstone to Stanmore, 2 July 1894, Paul Knaplund, ed., *Gladstone-Gordon Correspondence, 1851-1896*, Trans. American Philosophical Society, new series vol. 51 part 4, Philadelphia, 1961, 111).

[4] British Library ADD MS 44727, ff 256-257.

sometimes copied on loose sheets for easy reference.[1] 'Of the kind of correspondence properly called private and personal', he told Mrs. Cobden in 1865, 'I have none: indeed for many long years it has been out of my power, except in a very few instances, to keep up this kind of correspondence.'[2] This was somewhat of an exaggeration. He wrote hundreds of letters to his wife (1,537 survive at Hawarden, many of them of great political interest); and he also kept up correspondence with friends and close associates such as Lord Acton, Sir Thomas Dyke Acland, Owen Blayney Cole, James Hope-Scott and Cardinal Manning.

His predilection for the memorandum was not confined to his autobiographical writings. When in office he composed elaborate memoranda on a wide range of political topics, for circulation among Cabinet colleagues or submission to the Queen. She once received such a long and complex memorandum on the Irish Church that she had it shortened and clarified by her own staff before she grappled with it.[3] The habit extended into his correspondence. As Lathbury notes, Gladstone's letters 'not seldom have the air of memoranda, intended to clear his own mind, and then it is almost a matter of chance to whom they will be addressed'.[4] By contrast his journals or diaries, which he continued to keep in small note-books, contain for the most part brief factual entries.

He preserved a careful distinction between political and non-political work, having a desk for each in the library or Temple of Peace at Hawarden Castle. His non-political record-making was to a great extent literary. From 1831 onwards he wrote many notes headed 'Th', 'Hist', 'Philol', etc, ranging from summaries of books read to drafts for published works. His work on Homer was a major and long-lasting interest that generated a mound of papers, now mostly distributed by date through the 'Miscellanea' section of the Gladstone Papers in the British Library.[5]

---

[1] Sir Edward W. Hamilton, *Mr. Gladstone, a Monograph*, 1899, 81–83; [J. A. Godley,] *Reminiscences of Lord Kilbracken*, 1931, 87–88. The letter-books are now ADD MSS 44527–44551.

[2] Quoted in John Morley, *The Life of William Ewart Gladstone*, 1903, ii. 527.

[3] J. C. Beckett, 'Gladstone, Queen Victoria and the disestablishment of the Irish Church', *Irish Hist. Studies* XIII (1962–63), 38–47.

[4] D. C. Lathbury, ed., *Correspondence on Church and Religion of William Ewart Gladstone*, 1910, i.x.

[5] ADD MSS 44719–44776.

Gladstone's religious life was documented not only in his correspondence and diaries, but also in sermons read to his household[1] and devotions written for his own use during the Communion service.[2] Nor were mundane business and household records neglected. In 1838 he ceased to keep monthly accounts of income and expenditure, 'thinking that the advantage of the practice lies in the mental habit, which should by that time have been attained',[3] but he continued to keep summaries of his charitable and other expenditure.[4] He was once impressed, when calling on Peel when the latter was Prime Minister, to notice tradesmen's books 'laid on a desk seemingly as if for inspection'.[5] Here, as in other ways, the habits of commercial probity and evangelical strictness inherited from his father were reinforced by the example of his political mentor Peel.

The papers generated by Gladstone himself were greatly exceeded in quantity by the waves of incoming letters and papers that daily broke upon his desk. His method of dealing with them depended on whether he was in or out of office. When in office, and more particularly as Prime Minister, he could make use of a secretarial staff. Letters to him at 10 Downing Street were almost invariably acknowledged in some form, except when the correspondent was a known lunatic, but only about one tenth of each day's post-bag was selected for his personal attention, and not all of those received a reply in his own hand. The remaining nine-tenths were sorted into piles for the appropriate formal answer, and Gladstone would go through them very rapidly once a week, exclaiming 'Bosh . . . bosh!' as he skimmed through the ill-informed impertinences. At Hawarden he employed no paid secretary. In later years his sons acted as amanuenses, just as he himself had helped his ageing father in the 1840s. 'Correspondents did not get the encouragement generally supposed.' About ten of the fifty to one hundred letters received each day were answered by Gladstone himself (the majority by postcard), another ten were acknowledged by Henry

---

[1] ADD MSS 44779–44781.

[2] Now ADD MSS 44831, 44834; Lambeth Palace Library, MS 2758, ff 66–84.

[3] ADD MS 44804A.

[4] Five accompt books are now in the British Library (ADD MS 44804), and another five among the Glynne-Gladstone MSS.

[5] *W. E. Gladstone II: Autobiographical Memoranda 1832–1845*, 1972, 137.

Neville Gladstone or another member of the family, and the rest were left unacknowledged.[1]

The first archivist of the Gladstone papers was Gladstone himself. As early as 1822 he was keeping private papers in his personal closet in the room known as the Octagon at Seaforth House, his family home outside Liverpool.[2] Presumably he had the shape of that room in mind when, sixty-five years later, he designed a muniment room at Hawarden. During the 1830s, when he began to accumulate political as well as personal records, his diaries often contain entries such as 'Horrid confusion of papers: what a science it requires to keep them in order' (2 February 1836), or 'Arranging papers in my new box, which I hope will conduce to order' (7 November 1836). On 25 November 1837 he wrote a memorandum to define his practice. Of letters he stated: 'Let keeping be the general rule, only burn such scraps as cannot be subjects of interest or future reference'. Letters likely to be referred to again were separated from those of less use or interest, but everything (except the 'scraps') was to be made into bundles, labelled, and at the end of the year consigned for permanent storage. For current papers relating to specific topics Gladstone favoured the use of 'niches' or compartments.[3]

By the 1850s he had accumulated a great quantity of letters in monthly bundles, plus further correspondence among bundles of papers arranged by subject. In 1855 he began to construct a series of special correspondence, by extracting letters from both the chronological and the subject bundles. By 1867 this third series, alphabetically arranged by writer, seems to have had letters from some 320 correspondents.[4] Later, as Prime Minister, groups of papers accumulated for each of his periods of office. As well as general correspondence, and letters from ministerial colleagues, files were formed on departmental and fiscal matters, honours and appointments, ecclesiastical questions, and so on.[5]

---

[1] Hamilton, *op. cit.*, 81–83; Kilbracken, *op. cit.*, 87–88; Ivor Thomas, *Gladstone of Hawarden, a Memoir of Henry Neville, Lord Gladstone of Hawarden*, 1936, 94; Francis W. Hirst, *Gladstone as Financier and Economist*, 1931, 300–321 (chapter contributed by H. N. Gladstone).

[2] S. G. Checkland, *The Gladstones: A Family Biography 1764–1851*, 1971, 97.

[3] ADD MS 44727, ff 256–258; M. R. D. Foot and H. C. G. Matthew, ed., *The Gladstone Diaries*, 1968– , i. 358.

[4] ADD MS 44825.

[5] Glynne-Gladstone MSS A/41/6.

Only when he was out of office did he have much time to spare for arranging his papers. In 1888 a strong-room, the Octagon, was built on to the library at Hawarden Castle. It had shelved cupboards in two sections, above and below an iron gallery, and was of fireproof and burglar-proof construction. Unfortunately it was far from damp-proof, and when John Morley went to Hawarden only eleven years later he found some of the material there 'damp and faded'.[1]

By the time of Gladstone's death Hawarden Castle was crammed with his papers, not only in the Octagon but in cupboards and drawers in the Temple of Peace and elsewhere. The major categories were as follows:

1. Special and family correspondence, arranged by correspondent.
2. General correspondence, in monthly or alphabetical bundles.
3. Letter-books, registers of letters and loose copies of out-letters.
4. Political papers in subject bundles, including papers as Chancellor of the Exchequer and Prime Minister, together with papers as Special Commissioner for the Ionian Islands.
5. Diaries, travel journals, autobiographical memoranda and drafts for an autobiography.
6. Devotional writings and sermons.
7. Notes for speeches.
8. Literary papers, including notes and drafts for published works.
9. Personal, household and estate accounts and papers.
10. Trust and executorship papers, including papers as trustee for the 5th Duke of Newcastle.
11. Pamphlets, newspaper cuttings and other printed matter.

In his will Gladstone included among the heirlooms that were to pass with the estate 'autograph letters from her Majesty, and any other letters and papers of special interest which my Executors shall select for the purpose'.[2] All his other manuscript letters and papers he left absolutely to his executors, with full power to preserve, dispose of, or destroy them. The burden of the executorship fell on his sons Henry Neville (later Baron Gladstone of Hawarden) and Herbert (later

---

[1] [A. Tilney Bassett,] *The Gladstone Papers*, 1930, 3; Francis W. Hirst, *In the Golden Days*, 1947, 179 n. The Octagon was built by Douglas and Fordham of Chester for a little over £300 (Glynne-Gladstone MSS).

[2] ADD MS 44827.

Viscount Gladstone), and particularly on the former as the businessman of the family. Both laid great emphasis on safeguarding their father's political and personal reputation. Throughout their later years they devoted much time and thought to the preservation of the papers, and to making them available to approved biographers and editors.

The first of these was Morley. The mounds of papers that confronted him in 1899 were certainly formidable in quantity, but the care already bestowed on them made them far from unmanageable. Morley and his assistant F. W. Hirst sat in the library, and worked through papers produced from the Octagon by Miss Helen Gladstone. Hirst also looked at some of the general correspondence, but found it to be 'mostly rubbish'.[1] Selected documents were sent to Macmillans in London for transcription, where some of them accidentally remained until their discovery in 1969.[2]

Morley's work for his *Life of Gladstone* took 'four years of pretty vigorous exertion'.[3] He and Hirst had been thorough in the examination of the papers, but they were no archivists, and the papers were left in need of further sorting. This was done by Arthur Tilney Bassett (1869–1964), who by 1908 had completed a meticulous, if unimaginative, re-arrangement and cataloguing of the Octagon collection. The most important of Bassett's sections was a much expanded special correspondence, now over 47,000 letters from just over 2,000 correspondents, and stored in 230 boxes. A further 53 boxes were filled with Gladstone's out-letters, both copies and originals. 'Cabinet notes' occupied 4 boxes, notes for speeches 14 boxes, 'Notes and Memoranda' (that is, subject bundles with the correspondence extracted) 45 boxes, and literary drafts and notes 15 boxes. A mass of printed material, much of it annotated by Gladstone, was placed in another series of 75 boxes, and Bassett also tackled a quantity of general correspondence (about 30,000 letters, in 105 boxes) that he had found in the Octagon.[4] All the papers catalogued by Bassett were lodged in 1908 in a specially-constructed muniment room in St. Deiniol's Library, Hawarden. This Library and study centre had been Gladstone's own idea, and had been embodied in permanent buildings after his death as a memorial to him.

---

[1] Hirst, *In the Golden Days*, 180; Glynne-Gladstone MSS A/41/6.
[2] The papers were presented to the British Museum in 1970 by Sir William Gladstone, Bt., and are now ADD MSS 56444–56453. (See *Summary*, section C.)
[3] John, Viscount Morley, *Recollections*, 1917, ii. 92.
[4] For his catalogues see ADD MSS 44558–44562, 44714.

The papers catalogued by Bassett did not, however, comprise the entire Gladstone archive. Although Bassett catalogued the section of the general correspondence that he found in the Octagon, he did not give the same treatment to other sections of the general correspondence stored elsewhere in the Castle. He also omitted the Ionian papers, some of the more private papers such as the diaries, and nearly all the financial, legal, trust, estate and other business papers.

After completing his catalogue Bassett found additional material in Hawarden Castle, some of it literary and personal but some of it political. He appears, however, to have placed this material in the Octagon rather than in the St. Deiniol's Library muniment room. He also destroyed the sections of the general correspondence that had been stored outside the Octagon, having first extracted from them about a thousand letters from correspondents already represented in his catalogue.[1]

According to Bassett the British Museum had expressed interest in acquiring Gladstone's public and political papers as early as 1887.[2] But it was not until 1929 that negotiations were opened. Bassett went through the special correspondence, indicating for the Gladstone brothers certain sensitive or highly personal letters that they might think should be kept back. In the event, however, it seems to have been agreed that all the catalogued papers should be transferred to the Museum, to begin with as a loan, where Bassett as a temporary member of staff would sort through them and decide what should be returned to Hawarden. What remained in the Museum was to become an outright gift on the deaths of the executors, or on 1 January 1940 if either were still alive at that date. On 30 June 1930, therefore, the papers were placed in a pantechnicon and drawn by horse to Chester for despatch to London by rail, 'for their guardian would not take the risk of fire in a motor-driven vehicle'.[3]

They reached the Museum the following day, and Bassett began his work of re-sorting. Letters from members of Gladstone's family were extracted from Bassett's special correspondence for return to Hawarden, and a few other letters were also extracted because of their private nature. With these exceptions the special correspondence was retained, but in conformity with British Museum practice it was much reduced

---

[1] Glynne-Gladstone MSS Z/2.

[2] *The Gladstone Papers*, 5.

[3] Thomas, *Gladstone of Hawarden*, 240; British Museum, *Catalogue of Additions to the Manuscripts, The Gladstone Papers*, 1953, v.

in size, from over two thousand correspondents to two hundred. The remaining correspondences were then re-sorted by date to form a new 'general' correspondence. Of Bassett's original general correspondence, the hundred and five boxes that he had found in the Octagon and patiently catalogued,[1] only a small proportion was selected for retention in the Museum. For the memoranda and miscellaneous papers a chronological rather than a subject arrangement was adopted, thus completing the destruction of Gladstone's original subject bundles.

The bulk of the papers retained by the Museum became the property of the Nation in 1935, on the death of Lord Gladstone of Hawarden, the last surviving executor. But Bassett had put on one side the royal correspondence, since these letters, as heirlooms, could not form part of the gift. In 1931 they were constituted a separate group, to be held in the Museum on permanent loan from the tenant-for-life of the Gladstone settled estates.[2]

Before arranging for the transfer of the bulk of Gladstone's papers to the British Museum, his sons had found a solution to a problem that had been exercising them for several years. Stories affecting the private character of their father had long been circulating, and the brothers' campaign to defend his reputation culminated in the court case *Wright v Gladstone* in 1927. They gathered together a group of papers bearing on the case, which they referred to as the 'Arcana'. Most important were the journals, or diaries, forty-one small notebooks covering the period July 1825 to December 1896, which included references to Gladstone's habit of vigorous self-examination, his mode of private discipline, and his rescue work with prostitutes. There were also a few related private memoranda, and correspondence relating to the rescue work, principally with the rather 'fast' Mrs. Laura Thistlethwayte. The Gladstones wished to preserve the Arcana, realising that the diaries in particular were essential to an understanding of their father's life and character, but the problem was to find a suitable repository, and to prevent any partial or improper use of the papers. Following a suggestion by Cosmo Lang, then Archbishop of York, the material was handed over to the Archbishop of Canterbury in July 1928, for

---

[1] For the catalogue see ADD MS 44561.

[2] British Library MS Loans 73, summarily listed by the Commission in 1977 (NRA 21658). (See p. 128 below.)

preservation under the necessary safeguards in Lambeth Palace Library.[1]

At this stage the Gladstone brothers retained a transcript of the diaries, copies of other original material, papers concerning *Wright v Gladstone* received from their solicitor Sir Charles Russell, and their own more recent papers on the disposition of the Gladstone archive. In 1930 this supplementary material was placed in three tin boxes in the Octagon at Hawarden Castle and a special trust created for its supervision. When the trust was wound up in 1938 the solicitor's papers and newspaper cuttings relating to *Wright v Gladstone* (tin boxes B and C) were retained at Hawarden. The remainder (box A) was transferred to Lambeth and added to the earlier deposit.[2]

As a result of these dispositions the Gladstone papers were physically separated into four principal groups—the bulk of the public and political papers in the British Museum, the royal correspondence also in the British Museum but as a loan, the Arcana in Lambeth Palace Library and the remainder at Hawarden. The papers remaining at Hawarden were of a mixed nature, and among the family and business papers historians are sometimes surprised to find material closely related to the papers now in the British Library. This is because the Hawarden papers represent the results of three distinct archival processes. They comprise:

1. Personal, family, business and other papers excluded by Bassett from his catalogue of 1908.
2. Items of political interest found by Bassett after 1908 but not incorporated in the catalogued collection.
3. Catalogued papers sent to the British Museum in 1930, but returned to Hawarden.

After the transfer of the catalogued papers to the St. Deiniol's muniment room in 1908, the empty shelves of the Octagon soon began to fill with other material, much of it not part of W. E. Gladstone's own archive. By 1922 it contained deeds and legal papers for the Hawarden estate formerly housed in the old muniment room of the Castle, Glynne family papers, and Gladstone family papers. The last-named were later supplemented by additional material from Fasque, the Gladstone family's Scottish seat.

---

[1] Now Lambeth Palace Library MSS 1416–1455 (diaries) and 2758–2770. (See p. 129 below.)

[2] MSS 2771–2774.

In 1926 Henry Neville Gladstone deposited a collection of Hawarden deeds and legal papers in the National Library of Wales, and eight years later he made a further deposit of Glynne family papers, including one or two items relating to W. E. Gladstone.[1] Finally, in 1968–69, the remaining contents of the Octagon were transferred to St. Deiniol's Library muniment room, a transfer reminiscent of the previous emptying of the Octagon sixty years before.[2]

It was the wish of Gladstone's family in the early years of this century to publish as complete a record as possible of his life and work. Morley was the first official biographer, assisted in his research by F. W. Hirst and William Stead. But the result was an unbalanced *tour de force*, inevitably so in view of the exclusion of the religious side of Gladstone's life. The attempt to fill this gap, D. C. Lathbury's edition of the religious correspondence and papers, which came out in 1910, was a disappointment to Gladstone's sons. A selective edition of the speeches by Arthur Tilney Bassett followed in 1916, and after the war Gladstone's major achievements in Irish policy and public finance were chronicled by two approved Liberal historians of the younger generation, J. L. Hammond and F. W. Hirst. H. N. Gladstone added some personal recollections to Hirst's volume, and Viscount Gladstone marked the thirtieth anniversary of his father's death by an appreciation entitled *After Thirty Years*. But the full-scale biography of Gladstone the human figure by somebody who knew him well never materialised. Arthur Godley (Lord Kilbracken), a former private secretary, was approached by the brothers in 1906 and again in 1910, but declined on both occasions.[3]

Editions of Gladstone's major correspondence were eventually entrusted to Philip Guedalla, who published the correspondence with Palmerston in 1928, and the royal correspondence in 1933. The latter

---

[1] Francis Green, *Calendar of Deeds and Documents* [in the National Library of Wales], vol. 3, *The Hawarden Deeds*, 1931; National Library of Wales, *Annual Report 1934–1935*, 44.

[2] These papers, the property of Sir William Gladstone, Bt., are in the care of the County Archivist of Clwyd, who has acted as honorary archivist to St. Deiniol's Library since 1968. See *Guide to the Flintshire Record Office*, 1974, 127–140. The Clwyd Record Office holds some Hawarden estate papers, deposited by the Gladstone family solicitors in 1964, and the records of the Gladstone family firm now known as Ogilvy, Gillanders and Co. (NRA 9839, 14174). Some recent family and estate records remain at Fasque (NRA 10151).

[3] Kilbracken, *op. cit.*, 228.

was in part a response to the edition of Queen Victoria's later letters by G. E. Buckle, the Conservative editor of *The Times* and biographer of Disraeli. Gladstone's relations with the Queen, as is well known, deteriorated in their later years, a fact attributed by Herbert Gladstone primarily to the influence of Disraeli.[1] In 1936 Bassett brought out an edition of Gladstone's letters to his wife.

More recent editorial work includes Miss Ramm's volumes of Gladstone–Granville correspondence, the edition of the *Gladstone Diaries* now proceeding under the editorship of Dr. H. C. G. Matthew, and this Commission's edition of the autobiographical writings.

*Summary*

A. *British Library* ADD MSS 44086–44835. Correspondence and papers 1818–98. 750 volumes comprising:
Special correspondence. 266 vols.; general correspondence 1826–98. 175 vols.; letter-books 1835–94. 25 vols.; registers of letters received 1841–55. 6 vols.; papers relating to Cabinet meetings 1853–94. 13 vols.; official papers, mostly printed, 1834–95. 73 vols.; ecclesiastical patronage books 1868–74, 1880–86. 2 vols.; notes for speeches 1825–96. 32 vols.; autobiographical, political, literary and other memoranda and notes 1832–98. 68 vols.; literary manuscripts 1830–97. 33 vols.; Eton and Oxford papers, sermons, travel journals, accompts, guest lists, visiting books, devotional works c1818–1929. 49 vols.; catalogues and indexes of the papers 1864–1944. 8 vols.

B. *British Library* MS Loans 73. Royal correspondence 1845–97. 28 packets, comprising correspondence with Queen Victoria and her private secretaries, the Prince Consort and other members of the Royal Family.

C. *British Library* ADD MSS 56444–56453. (Papers removed from Hawarden in connection with the preparation of Morley's *Life*.) 10 volumes of correspondence and papers comprising:
Correspondence and papers relating to Ireland, Egypt and the Sudan 1880–91. 7 vols.; miscellaneous correspondence and papers 1845–1902, including correspondence relating to the Newark seat

---

[1] Viscount Gladstone, *After Thirty Years*, 1928, 351 ff.

1845–46 and the Midlothian seat 1879, political memoranda and papers 1880–97, original letters from WEG to the 7th Earl Cowper 1880–81, and letters to Viscount Morley. 3 vols.

D. *British Library* ADD MS 46044. (Viscount Gladstone papers.) One volume, comprising correspondence of WEG relating to H. J. Gladstone's candidature for Leeds 1874–80, and papers of H. J. Gladstone as private secretary to his father 1881–85.

E. *British Library* ADD MS 46221. (Mary Drew papers.) One volume, comprising family letters to and from WEG 1850–97.

F. *Lambeth Palace Library* MSS 1416–1455, 2758–2774. Journals and related papers 1825–1936. 57 volumes comprising:
Journals 1825–96. 41 vols. bound as 40; correspondence relating to rescue work with prostitutes 1845–96. 1 vol.; correspondence with Laura Thistlethwayte 1865–93. 10 vols.; personal memoranda and devotional writings *c*1836–57. 1 vol.; later papers *c*1913–36. 5 vols.
*Note.* Material cannot be made publicly available until it has been published in the relevant volume of *The Gladstone Diaries*.

G. *St. Deiniol's Library, Hawarden:* Glynne–Gladstone MSS. Personal, family, business and miscellaneous papers *c*1817–98. *c*50,000 items including:
Family correspondence, including letters to W. E. Gladstone 1821–98, and letters from him to his wife (1839–94) and other members of his family; correspondence relating to his proposal of marriage to Miss Caroline Farquhar 1835–36; miscellaneous, minor and anonymous correspondence *c*1837–96. 109 boxes; letters from WEG to O. B. and F. B. O. Cole 1832–95, Sir John Cowan 1877–94, Lady F. Cavendish 1882–91 and others; letters of congratulation and condolence 1835–98; political and personal memoranda 1833–94; accompts and correspondence relating to Newark elections 1832–45; appointments diary 1886; Ionian Islands papers 1852–63. 3 boxes; accompt books (7 vols.), bank books and financial papers 1832–97; legal, trusteeship and executorship papers (5th Duke of Newcastle and others); estate and household papers; literary papers *c*1845–94; press cuttings and other printed matter. 26 boxes; papers of Horace

Seymour (private secretary) 1880–1901; correspondence of Sir Edward Hamilton 1880–87; papers relating to WEG's death, the disposition of his archive, etc, *c*1898–1940.

*Note.* Enquiries regarding these papers should be addressed to the County Archivist, Clwyd Record Office, The Old Rectory, Hawarden, Deeside, Clwyd. For further details see the *Guide to the Flintshire Record Office*, 1974. A full catalogue is in course of preparation (1979).

# TABLE OF SOURCES, W. E. GLADSTONE I–IV

GLADSTONE PAPERS. The British Library

BL ADD MS 44093   *Correspondence with Lord Acton 1860–1887*
ff 209–214   WEG to Acton. 26 January 1880. IV, 44–45.
ff 215–217   WEG to Acton. 6 March 1880. IV, 45.
ff 219–220   Acton to WEG. 11 March 1880. IV, 46–47.
ff 223–225   WEG to Acton. 14 March 1880. IV, 47–48.
ff 300–301   Acton to WEG. 16 August 1887. I, 2–3.

BL ADD MS 44140   *Correspondence with the 14th Earl of Derby and others*
f 172   Stanley to WEG. 22 February [1851]. III, 71n.
ff 192–193   WEG to Derby. 31 January 1855. III, 158.
ff 205–207   Derby to WEG. 25 January 1857. III, 210–211.
ff 208–209   WEG to Derby. 26 January 1857. III, 211–212.
f 210   WEG to Derby. 31 January 1857. III, 212.
f 211   Derby to WEG. 31 January 1857. III, 212–213.
ff 221–226   Derby to WEG. [23 January 1857.] III, 218–220.

BL ADD MS 44161   *Correspondence with George Joachim Goschen, later 1st Viscount Goschen*
ff 339–340   Goschen to WEG (extract). 11 June 1894. III, 254n.

BL ADD MS 44163   *Correspondence with Sir James Graham 1837–1855*
ff 55–56   WEG to Graham. 27 March 1852. III, 125.
ff 57–59   Graham to WEG. 29 March 1852. III, 125–126.
ff 60–61   WEG to Graham. 30 March 1852. III, 126.

BL ADD MS 44164   *The same 1856–1861*
ff 30–32   WEG to Graham, with enclosure. 16 June 1856. III, 208n., 207n.
ff 165–172   Graham to WEG. 25 May 1858. III, 225–227.

BL ADD MS 44275   *Correspondence with Sir Robert Peel 1834–1850*
f 102   Peel to WEG. 6 February 1842. I, 234.
ff 104–105   WEG to Peel. 6 February 1842. I, 234–235.
f 106   Peel to WEG. 6 February 1842. I, 235.
ff 140–141   Peel to WEG. 13 May 1843. II, 196–197.
ff 142–143   WEG to Peel. 14 May 1843. II, 200–201.

BL ADD MS 44291    *Correspondence with Lord John Russell 1849–1860*
f 312          Russell to WEG. 20 May 1860. III, 230.


BL ADD MS 44335    *Correspondence with Sir George Otto Trevelyan 1867–1895*
ff 216–217    WEG to Trevelyan. [24 May 1887.] IV, 84–85.


BL ADD MS 44339    *Correspondence with Gerald Valerian Wellesley, Dean of Windsor, 1852–1871*
ff 9–10       Wellesley to WEG. 24 March 1862. III, 244.


BL ADD MS 44358    *General correspondence April–December 1841*
ff 56–57      WEG to Lord Robert Grosvenor. 8 July 1841. II, 150–151.
ff 145–146    WEG to the Editor of the *Morning Advertiser*. 8 October 1841. II, 165–166.


BL ADD MS 44359    *General correspondence 1842*
ff 117–120    The Rev. Nicholas Wiseman to WEG. 6 June 1842. II, 179–181.
f 121         WEG to the Rev. Nicholas Wiseman. 7 June 1842. II, 181–182.


BL ADD MS 44385    *General correspondence January–May 1856*
ff 285–286    WEG to Edward Ellice. 4 April 1856. III, 204–205.
ff 291–292    Edward Ellice to WEG. 5 April 1856. III, 205–206.


BL ADD MS 44386    *General correspondence June–December 1856*
ff 30–31      Henry James Baillie to WEG. [17 June 1856.] III, 209n.


BL ADD MS 44491    *General correspondence June–July 1885*
ff 122–125    A. J. Balfour to WEG. 16 June 1885. IV, 68–69.


BL ADD MS 44500    *General correspondence January–May 1887*
ff 269–271    Edwin Hodder to WEG (extract). 29 April 1887. III, 262.
ff 273–274    WEG to Edwin Hodder. 30 April 1887. III, 262–263.


BL ADD MS 44509    *General correspondence January–April 1890*
f 241         Professor John Tyndall to WEG. 9 March 1890. IV, 87.

BL ADD MS 44527   *Letter-book 1835–1844*
f 37          WEG to Sir Thomas Fremantle. 8 October 1841. II, 165.

BL ADD MS 44641   *Papers relating to Cabinet meetings 1873–1874*
f 64          WEG's notes of the meeting of 12 March 1873. IV, 29.
ff 74–75      WEG's notes of the meeting of 13 March 1873. IV, 30–31.

BL ADD MS 44721   *Memoranda and notes 1831–1832*
ff 20–21      WEG's anti-Reform handbills of 1831. I, 230–231.

BL ADD MS 44722   *Memoranda 1832–1833*
ff 57–58      Poem entitled 'A Sunday Journey'. 14 October 1832. II, 31–34.

BL ADD MS 44724   *Memoranda January–October 1835*
f 51          Poem entitled 'To Violets in a Vaudois Valley'. March 1832. I, 232–233.
ff 164–175    'Recollections of the last hours of my mother.' 7–23 September 1835. II, 53–61.

BL ADD MS 44727   *Memoranda 1837*
ff 176–177    Biographical notes on Sir John Gladstone. September 1837. II, 82–83.

BL ADD MS 44730   *Memoranda 1842–1845*
ff 127–128    Conversation with Helen Gladstone on her religious position. 11 June 1842. II, 177–179.

BL ADD MS 44731   *Memoranda 1842*
ff 44–56      'Twenty-seven propositions relating to current questions in theology.' 29 December 1842. I, 236–245.

BL ADD MS 44732   *Memoranda 1843*
ff 141–142    'Memorandum . . . made for interview with Sir Robert Peel.' 13 May 1843. II, 197–198.

BL ADD MS 44735   *Memoranda 1845–1846*

f 20      WEG's review of his religious and political position.
          18 September 1845. II, 280–281.

ff 77–82  Conversation with Dr. Döllinger. 3 October 1845. III,
          1–6.

ff 83–88  Further notes on the previous conversation. 3 October
          1845. III, 6–8.

ff 89–92  Conversation with Father Hasslacher, a Jesuit, of Stras-
          bourg. 20 October 1845. III, 8–11.


BL ADD MS 44738   *Memoranda 1850*

ff 122–146 'Some account of our second daughter, Catherine Jessy
          Gladstone.' April 1850. III, 50–66.


BL ADD MS 44739   *Memoranda 1851*

ff 1–4    Conversations with Neapolitan political prisoners. 13
          February 1851. III, 66–70.

ff 104–120 'The Last Days of my Father, Sir John Gladstone. 1851.'
          November–December 1851. III, 80–102.


BL ADD MS 44741   *Memoranda January–March 1853*

ff 59–60  'Charges current against WEG.' January 1853. III, 131.

f 80      Conversation with Prince Albert and Cabinet discussion:
          WEG's first Budget. 9 April 1853. III, 131–132.


BL ADD MS 44745   *Memoranda 1855*

ff 22–29  Cabinet discussions following Lord John Russell's resigna-
          tion. 24–25 January 1855. III, 153–155. (Incorrectly
          cited on page 153 as ADD MS 44778, ff 22–29.)

f 30      Note on the Cabinet's decision to adjourn the House of
          Commons. 25 January 1855. III, 155.

ff 31–32  Lord John Russell's statement to the House of Commons on
          his resignation. 26 January 1855. III, 155–156.

ff 35–38  Memorandum on Lord Palmerston's accession to the
          Premiership. 4 and 5 February 1855. III, 168–169.

ff 39–46  Peelite discussion on a juncture with Lord Palmerston.
          5 February 1855. III, 170–172.

ff 47–55  The same; WEG's acceptance of office. 6 February 1855.
          III, 172–175.

ff 19–21,   Resolutions on the Budget. February 1857. III, 215n.,
29–30    217–218.

ff 169–175  An offer of Cabinet office from Lord Derby. 22 May 1858.
III, 221–224.

BL ADD MS 44752  *Memoranda 1862–1863*
ff 25–35    Conversation with the Queen: the late Prince Consort.
19 March 1862. III, 238–244.

BL ADD MS 44755  *Memoranda 1866–1867*
ff 90–92   Conversations with Lord John Russell and the Queen: the
defeat of the Reform Bill. 26 June 1866. III, 245–246.

ff 101–104  Conversation with Pope Pius IX. 22 October 1866. III,
246–250.

BL ADD MS 44756  *Memoranda 1868*
ff 59–60   Conversation with Lord Halifax: WEG invited to form a
Ministry. 28 November 1868. IV, 1–2.

ff 61–62   Conversation with General Grey: the position of Lord
Clarendon. 2 December 1868. IV, 2–3.

ff 63–64   Projected memorandum for the Queen: assurances to be
given by Lord Clarendon. 2 December 1868. IV, 2.

f 65    Conversation with General Grey: WEG's impressions of
Grey. 3 December 1868. IV, 3.

ff 67–68   Audience with the Queen: the new Ministry. 5 December
1868. IV, 4–5.

ff 69–70   Audience with the Queen: the new Ministry. 3 December
1868. IV, 4.

BL ADD MS 44758  *Memoranda 1869–1870*
ff 1–14   Negotiations on the Lords' amendments to the Irish
Church Bill. 17–22 July 1869. IV, 6–15.

BL ADD MS 44760  *Memoranda 1871–1872*
ff 40–45   Conversation with the Queen: a royal residence in Ireland.
25 June 1871. IV, 17–19.

ff 129–136  Conversation with the Queen: service of thanksgiving for
the recovery of the Prince of Wales. 21 December 1871.
IV, 22–25.

BL ADD MS 44761   *Memoranda 1873*

ff 100–101   Resignation and resumption of office. 12–16 March 1873. IV, 26–28.

ff 102–108   Events following the resignation of the Ministry. 13 March 1873. IV, 32–33.

BL ADD MS 44762   *Memoranda 1874–1875*

f 28   Audience with the Queen: the resignation of Ministers. 17 February 1874. IV, 34–35.

BL ADD MS 44763   *Memoranda 1876–1879*

ff 130–131   Conversation with Lord Carnarvon: the Queen's relations with her Cabinet. 25 May 1878. IV, 35–36.

ff 164–165   WEG's itinerary of his first Midlothian campaign, with an estimate of the size of his audiences. 24 November–8 December 1879. IV, 36–37.

BL ADD MS 44764   *Memoranda 1880*

ff 1–10   'Memorandum on the religious profession of my sister Helen Jane Gladstone.' 8 February 1880. IV, 37–44.

ff 43–47   Conversation with Lord Hartington: Hartington's audience with the Queen. 22 April 1880. IV, 48–50.

ff 48–49   Conversation with Lords Granville and Hartington: WEG summoned to Windsor. 23 April 1880. IV, 50–51.

ff 50–55   Audience with the Queen: WEG commissioned to form a Ministry. 23 April 1880. IV, 52–54.

BL ADD MS 44766   *Memoranda mostly 1882*

ff 6–7   WEG's health: memorandum for Dr. Clark. 7 January 1883. IV, 62–63.

ff 71–72   Conversation with Captain O'Shea: Parnell and the Irish Party. 5 May 1882. IV, 58–59.

ff 75–76   Memorandum by Catherine Gladstone of a conversation with Lady Derby: an invitation to Lord Derby to join the Cabinet. 18 May 1882. IV, 60.

ff 77–80   Conversation with Lady Derby: a further overture to Lord Derby. 24 May 1882. IV, 60–62.

f 117   WEG on the Conservative Party. 14 August 1882. IV, 103.

f 150   Audience with the Queen: ministerial appointments. 11 December 1882. IV, 62.

BL ADD MS 44767 *Memoranda 1883*

f 1     'Sleep Register.' January 1883. IV, 63.

ff 131–133     Conversation with Lord Hartington: Reform and Redistribution. 31 December 1883. IV, 64–65.

BL ADD MS 44768   *Memoranda 1884*

f 137     Note given to Sir Stafford Northcote. 13 November 1884. IV, 66n.

ff 146–147     Conversation with Sir Stafford Northcote: Reform and Redistribution. 13 November 1884. IV, 65–66.

BL ADD MS 44769   *Memoranda 1885*

f 35     Conservatism. 28 February 1885. IV, 103.

ff 129–131     Conversation with Arthur James Balfour: Lord Salisbury's attempt to form a Ministry. 16 June 1885. IV, 67–68.

f 132     Draft of WEG's reply to a letter from A. J. Balfour. 16 June 1885. IV, 69.

ff 135–136     Conversation with the Queen: the political crisis. 18 June 1885. IV, 69.

ff 138–139     Visit from Sir Henry Ponsonby. 20 June 1885. IV, 71.

ff 140–144     Interviews with Sir Henry Ponsonby. 22 June 1885. IV, 71–73.

ff 154–155     WEG's statement of the constitutional position. *c* 18 June 1885. IV, 70–71.

ff 167–168     'Memorandum submitted by Mr. Gladstone to Her Majesty at Windsor'. 18 June 1885. IV, 70.

BL ADD MS 44770   *Memoranda 1885–1887*

f 4     WEG on Toryism. 10 December 1885. IV, 104.

BL ADD MS 44771   *Memoranda January–March 1886*

ff 29–33     Interviews relating to the formation of WEG's third Ministry. 30 January 1886. IV, 73–75.

ff 46–47     The same. 31 January 1886. IV, 75–76.

ff 51–52     The same. 3 February 1886. IV, 76–77.

f 57     The same. 4 February 1886. IV, 77.

f 60     The same. 5 February 1886. IV, 77–78.

f 62     The same. 6 February 1886. IV, 78.

BL ADD MS 44772   *Memoranda March–December 1886*

f 1            Memorandum on a letter of rebuke from the Queen. 16 March 1886. IV, 78.

ff 111–117   Conversation with Sir Henry Ponsonby: the progress of the Home Rule Bill. 17 May 1886. IV, 79–80.

BL ADD MS 44773   *Memoranda 1887–1891*

ff 12–14     Gladstone's notes on Hodder's *Life of Shaftesbury*. III, 261–262.

ff 35–38     Conversation with Joseph Chamberlain: Irish policy. 5 April 1887. IV, 80–82.

ff 41–42     Conversation with Sir George Otto Trevelyan: retention of Irish Members at Westminster. 25 May 1887. IV, 82–83.

ff 46–47     Comments on a letter by Professor Tyndall: WEG and Home Rule. *post* 8 June 1887. IV, 85–86.

ff 48–50     Conversation with Charles Stewart Parnell. 10 March 1888. IV, 87–88.

ff 170–171   Charles Stewart Parnell's visit to Hawarden: Liberal policy on Ireland. 18–19 December 1889. IV, 89–90.

f 195        Conservatism and reverence. n.d. IV, 104.

f 210        Conversation with John Morley: the Irish Nationalists. 15 January 1891. IV, 91.

ff 234–235   WEG's reaction to the Tranby Croft case. *post* 9 June 1891. IV, 91.

BL ADD MS 44774   *Memoranda 1892*

ff 163–164   Audience with the Queen. 25 November 1892. IV, 92.

BL ADD MS 44776   *Memoranda 1894–1897*

ff 51–52     WEG's resignation: notes for a conversation with Sir Henry Ponsonby. 21 February 1894. IV, 92–93.

ff 57–58     Audience with the Queen: WEG's intended retirement. 28 February 1894. IV, 93–94.

ff 59–60     Final audience with the Queen. 3 March 1894. IV, 94–96.

ff 61–62     The Queen's reception of WEG's resignation. 28 February–3 March 1894. IV, 96–97.

ff 63–64     WEG's relations with the Queen. 10 and 11 March 1894. IV, 98.

ff 65–66     The same. 19 March 1894. IV, 98–99.

ff 67–68     WEG as the Sicilian mule. 20 March 1894. IV, 99–100.

ff 81–84     The Eton Debating Society. 29 June 1894. IV, 101–102.

ff 145–153   'Memorandum of proceedings in 1880 with relation to the unfulfilled covenants of the Treaty of Berlin.' (Extract.) III, 255–256.

ff 177–189   'Financial arrangements of 1853 as affecting Ireland.' III, 269–270.

ff 191–194   The renewal of the income tax in 1853. III, 270–273.


BL ADD MS 44777   *Political and autobiographical memoranda 1832–1851*

ff 1–12      Canvassing at Newark. September–October 1832. II, 3–20.

ff 13–14     Visit to the Duke of Newcastle at Clumber. 9 October 1832. II, 21–23.

ff 15–22     Conversations with the Duke of Newcastle. 9–10 October 1832. II, 24–31.

ff 23–28     Visit to Sir Robert Peel at Drayton Manor. 18–25 January 1836. II, 61–66.

f 29         Conversation with Samuel Rogers. 24 June 1836. II, 71–72.

ff 31–35     Visit to Lord Aberdeen at Haddo House. 27–29 October 1836. II, 72–75.

ff 36–39     Political and phrenological discussions. 5–6 December 1837. II, 84–86.

ff 40–51     A party at Sir Robert Peel's and a subsequent conversation. 9–13 December 1837. II, 86–90.

ff 52–53     Conversations with Samuel Rogers and Lord Aberdeen. 14–15 December 1837. II, 91.

ff 54–59     Sir John Eardley Wilmot's motion on negro apprenticeship. 22–24 May 1838. II, 103–105.

ff 60–62     Discussions on China; anecdotes of the royal family. 24–25 March 1840. II, 119–120.

ff 63–64     Thomas Grenville's account of the religious activities of the Rev. the Hon. George Spencer. 28 August 1840. II, 129–131.

ff 139–148 Conversations with Lord Stanley and Henry Goulburn on WEG's position in relation to the Maynooth grant. 4–5 March 1844. II, 244–249.

ff 149–150 Further note on the conversation with Lord Stanley; Cabinet meeting on Indian affairs, the Factory Bill and the Corn Laws. 4–16 March 1844. II, 249–250.

ff 151–154 'Memorandum on the position of the Government after the divisions on the Factory Bill.' 23 March 1844. II, 251–253.

ff 155–158 Cabinet discussion on the Factory Bill. 25 March 1844. II, 253–255.

ff 159–160 Further notes on a conversation with Lord Stanley; conversation with Sir James Graham on the Factory Bill. 4–23 March 1844. II, 255.

ff 161–162 Thomas Wyse's motion on Catholic education in Ireland. 2 March 1844. II, 242.

ff 165–166 Conversation with Sir Robert Peel on Irish ecclesiastical affairs. 1 March 1844. II, 237–238.

ff 168–171 Cabinet meeting on Indian affairs. 2 April 1844. II, 255–257.

ff 172–175 Cabinet meeting on the same; the Irish situation. 22–28 April 1844. II, 257–259.

ff 184–185 Cabinet changes. 30 April–16 May 1844. II, 259–260.

ff 186–187 Conversation with Lord Stanley on the younger political generation; John Lockhart's opinion of Newman. 20–30 May 1844. II, 260.

ff 188–193 Cabinet meetings after the Government's defeat on the sugar duties motion; discussion on the same with Lord Mahon. 15–17 June 1844. II, 261–264.

ff 194–195 Cabinet meeting on the same; Sir Robert Peel's Parliamentary conduct. 17–20 June 1844. II, 264–265.

ff 199–203 Conversation with Sir Robert Peel on Irish education; Cabinet meeting on the same and other questions. 8 July 1844. II, 265–267.

ff 204–205 Speeches in the House by Thomas Wyse and Sir Robert Peel on Irish education. 19 July 1844. II, 268.

ff 206–209 Cabinet meeting on Irish Collegiate education and the Maynooth grant. 19 November 1844. II, 269–271.

BL ADD MS 44790    *Autobiographica, written 1890–1894*

BL ADD MS 44791   *Autobiographica, written 1894–1897*
ff 1–19      'Early religious opinions.' I, 140–148.
f 20         'Political life considered as a profession.' I, 138–139.
f 21         Further list of critics. I, 254–255.
f 22         'Incidental to Resignation.' 1894–1896. I, 168–169.
ff 23–28     '1894. The final imbroglio.' 1893–1894. I, 117–120.
ff 29–44     'Recorded errors.' 1838–1892. I, 125–136.
ff 45–48     'Mistakes—certain, doubtful or suppositious.' I, 250–253.
ff 49–50     'Chief heads of legislative work.' 1842–1893. I, 137–138.
f 51         'General retrospect': reflexions on political insight. I, 136.
ff 53–54     'Latest visit to Windsor.' 3 March 1894. I, 169–171.
ff 55–56     'Crisis of 1894 as to the Lords and dissolution.' I, 115–117.
ff 57–63     'Cannes in 1897': a meeting with the Queen. I, 171–175.
ff 64–67     Recollections of Dr. John Keate. I, 26–28.
f 68         Childhood. I, 22–23.
f 69         Old age. I, 175.
ff 70–102    'Early Parliamentary Life, 1832–1852', including 'My first book.' I, 53–72.
ff 103–130   'Second stage of Parliamentary Life, 1853–1865.' I, 76–91.
ff 131–166   Later political life. 1865–1886. I, 91–112.

BL ADD MS 44792   *Miscellaneous undated memoranda*
f 196        The old Conservative school. IV, 104.

BL ADD MS 44819   *'Secret Political Memoranda' 1833–1843*
f 2          WEG's liability to distortion in his memoranda. 26 April 1836. II, 67–68.
f 2          Lord Stanley's conduct in relation to the apprenticeship clause in the Abolition of Slavery Act. 19 November 1837. II, 83–84.
f 3          The Abolition of Slavery Bill: modification of the apprenticeship clause. 24–25 July 1833. II, 34–35.
f 3          Conversation with a Peer [?Lord Manvers]. 9 July 1834. II, 35.
ff 3–5       Conversation with Daniel O'Connell. 10 July 1834. II, 35–36.
f 5          Anecdote of William Cobbett. 15 July 1834. II, 36–37.
f 5          A rumoured offer of the Privy Seal to Lord Grey. 21 July 1834. II, 37.

ff 5–7 Conversations with Sir Robert Peel and others. 29 July 1834. II, 37–38.

f 7 Peel's position in July 1834, as reported by Lord Lincoln. 1 August 1834. II, 38–39.

f 7 Political anecdotes. October 1834. II, 39.

ff 7–8 Interview with Sir Robert Peel: WEG's acceptance of office as a Lord of the Treasury. 20 December 1834. II, 39–40.

f 9 Dinner at Lord Lyndhurst's: anecdotes of Lord Brougham. 17 January 1835. II, 40–41.

ff 9–11 Interview with Sir Robert Peel: WEG's acceptance of office as Under Secretary for the Colonies. 26 January 1835. II, 41–43.

ff 11–12 Conversation with Charles Canning on his political career. 3 February 1835. II, 43–44.

ff 13–14 Anecdotes of Lords Brougham, Melbourne and Palmerston. 17 February 1835. II, 44–46.

f 14 Defeat of the Government on the Speakership. 20 February 1835. II, 46.

ff 14–15 Political conversations. 23 and 26 February 1835. II, 46–47.

ff 15–17 Resignation of Sir Robert Peel. 8 April 1835. II, 47–49.

ff 17–19 Views of the Conservative leaders on leaving office. 13–15 April 1835. II, 49–51.

ff 19–20 Anecdotes of Peel's religious principles. 28 March 1835. II, 51–52.

f 20 Conversation with Sir Edward Kerrison on the dissolution of December 1834. 1835. II, 52.

f 21 Peel's opinions on the Reform Bill and the Municipal Corporations Bill. 19 June–3 August 1835. II, 52.

ff 21–22 Conversation with Lady Canning. 6 February 1836. II, 66–67.

f 22 WEG revises his former opinion of Lord Aberdeen. 12 February 1836. II, 67.

ff 22–23 WEG on George Canning, Lord Londonderry and Thomas Buxton. 26 April 1836. II, 68–69.

ff 24–25 Conversations with William Wordsworth, Thomas Noon Talfourd and Richard Sheil. 30 May–8 June 1836. II, 69–71.

ff 26–30 Conversations on politics and religion. 4–16 March 1837. II, 75–81.

ff 30–31 Conversation with Sir Henry Hardinge on the Irish Municipal Corporations Bill. 11 April 1837. II, 81–82.

f 31 Anecdotes of Bishop Phillpotts and Lord Grey. 8–13 June 1837. II, 82.

f 32 Interview with the Duke of Wellington. 28 November 1837. II, 84.

ff 32–33 Meetings at Sir Robert Peel's. 16–20 January 1838. II, 91–93.

ff 33–34 The Lower Canada Government Bill. 20–25 January 1838. II, 93.

f 34 Sir William Molesworth's motion of no confidence in Lord Glenelg. 16–17 February 1838. II, 94.

ff 34–37 Further discussions on the same. 26–27 February 1838. II, 94–99.

ff 37–38 The same. 3–5 March 1838. II, 99–100.

f 38 Conversation on the rupture between Canning and the Tory party. 11 April 1838. II, 100.

f 38 Conversation with Sir James Graham on ecclesiastical questions. 22 April 1838. II, 100–101.

ff 38–39 Conversation with Samuel Rogers. 25 April 1838. II, 101.

f 39 Anecdotes of Lord Brougham, Lord Stanley, and the King of Hanover. 28 March–25 April 1838. II, 102.

ff 39–40 Discussions on Ireland at Sir Robert Peel's. 19 May 1838. II, 102.

f 40 Discussions on the Scottish Church Extension Bill. 12 June 1838. II, 105–106.

ff 40–41 Anecdotes of Sir Robert Peel. 13–22 June 1838. II, 107.

ff 41–42 The Irish Tithe Bill. 17–18 July 1838. II, 108.

f 42 Further discussions on the same. 25 July 1838. II, 109–110.

ff 43–44 Conversation with Baron Bunsen on religion in Europe. 1 March 1839. II, 110–111.

f 44 Conversations on religious matters. 18–19 March 1839. II, 112.

f 45 Conversation with Charles de Montalembert on the same. 23 March 1839. II, 112–113.

ff 45–46 A party at Sir Stratford Canning's; conversation with Sir Robert Peel. 6–18 April 1839. II, 113–114.

ff 46–47 | The Bedchamber crisis; the history of the Jamaica Government Bill. 25 March–7 May 1839. II, 114–116.

f 48 | The Bedchamber crisis. 6–11 May 1839. II, 116–117.

f 48 | Sir John Buller's motion of no confidence. 16 January 1840. II, 117.

ff 48–49 | Conversations with James Hope and Sir Robert Peel. 17–18 March 1840. II, 117–119.

ff 49–51 | Conversations on Canada. 9–13 June 1840. II, 120–122.

ff 51–52 | The Canadian Clergy Reserves Bill. 15 June 1840. II, 123–124.

f 52 | Lord Morpeth's amendment to the Irish Voters' Bill. 19 June 1840. II, 124–125.

f 52 | Further discussion on the Canadian Clergy Reserves Bill. 20 June 1840. II, 125.

f 53 | The same. 24 June 1840. II, 125–126.

ff 53–54 | Discussions on the Canadian Clergy Reserves Bill and the British Guiana Civil List. 27–30 June 1840. II, 126–127.

ff 54–55 | Sir Robert Inglis's motion on Church Extension; conversation with Colonel John Gurwood. 30 June–1 July 1840. II, 127–128.

f 55 | Discussion with Sir Thomas Dyke Acland on Parliamentary grants for education. 20 July 1840. II, 129.

f 55 | Anecdotes of Lord John Russell and the Duke of Wellington. 1840. II, 129.

f 56 | Anecdotes of Sir Robert Peel and Lord John Russell. 23–31 March 1841. II, 131.

f 56 | The same. 7 May 1841. II, 137–138.

f 56 | Conservative tactics on the sugar duties question. 3–4 May 1841. II, 134.

ff 57–61 | The state of affairs in politics and religion. 9 May 1841. II, 135–137.

f 61 | WEG's speech in Parliament on sugar duties. 10 May 1841. II, 138.

f 61 | Ministerial tactics. 15 May 1841. II, 138–139.

ff 61–63 | Conservative discussions on the political crisis. 11–22 May 1841. II, 141–143.

ff 63–64 | François Rio on Daniel O'Connell; the defeat of the Government. 3–5 June 1841. II, 146–147.

ff 100–102   Cabinet meetings on Ireland and education. 11–17 June 1843. II, 205–208.

ff 102–103   Cabinet meetings on Irish spirit duties and Indian affairs. 20–24 June 1843. II, 208–209.

ff 103–104   Sir Robert Peel's handling of the Cabinet; his view on current questions. 24–27 June 1843. II, 209–210.

ff 104–105   Cabinet meeting on Canadian and Indian affairs. 1 July 1843. II, 210–211.

ff 105–106   Cabinet meeting on Indian affairs. 4 July 1843. II, 211–212.

ff 106–107   Cabinet meeting on Irish affairs, Lord Brougham's Bill for the suppression of the slave trade, and duelling. 8 August 1843. II, 218–219.

ff 107–108   A meeting at Sir Robert Peel's on foreign and commercial policy. 16 August 1843. II, 219–220.

BL ADD MS 56445   *Miscellaneous correspondence and papers 1855–1897, unfoliated*
Conversation with Musurus Pasha, Turkish Ambassador in London. 14 May 1880. IV, 54–57.
Conversation with Aristarchi Bey, Turkish Attaché at Paris. 21 May 1880. IV, 57–58.
Conversation with Count Münster, German Ambassador in London: the Eastern Question. 1 October 1880. IV, 58.
'Autobiographica. 1881': Turkey's cession of Thessaly to Greece. October 1880. Written 1894. III, 252–254.
'Second cabinet of 1880–5.' III, 256–260.

BL ADD MS 56448   *Papers relating to the Parnell affair November 1890, unfoliated*
Conversation with Justin McCarthy: relations with Parnell following the O'Shea divorce. 30 November 1890. IV, 90.

BL ADD MS 56451   *Papers relating to General Gordon and the Sudan 1884–1885, unfoliated*
Cabinet meetings on the Sudan. 10–30 March 1884. IV, 65.

GLYNNE–GLADSTONE mss. St. Deiniol's Library, Hawarden.[1]

*Correspondence of WEG with his father Sir William Gladstone*
Draft, WEG to his father. 7 January 1832. I, 220–229.


ABERDEEN PAPERS. The British Library.

BL ADD MS 43071 *Correspondence with WEG 1854–1860*
ff 285–290 WEG to Aberdeen. 13 March 1856. III, 195–199.


FARR PAPERS. John Rylands University Library of Manchester.

ENGLISH MS 339 *Correspondence of William Windham Farr (1808–87) 1826–1832*
WEG to Farr. 17 October 1826, 31 October 1826, 22 November 1826, 15 March 1827, 29 March 1827, 15 May 1827, 22 May 1827, 3 July 1827, 5 September 1827, 14 September 1827, 26 November 1827, 23 January 1828, 11 March 1828, 5 May 1828, 25 September 1828, 29 October 1828, 26 January 1829, 17 November 1829, 4 February 1830, 2 June 1830, 5 July 1830, 13 September 1830, 21 December [1832]. I, 179–219.


SIR EDWARD HAMILTON PAPERS. The British Library.

BL ADD MS 48642 *Diary of Sir Edward Walter Hamilton 8 November 1885–6 February 1886*
ff 113–136 29 January–6 February 1886. IV, 105–117.


PALMERSTON PAPERS. Broadlands mss.[2]

GC/RU *Correspondence with Lord John Russell*
600 Russell to Palmerston. 20 May 1860. III, 231–232.
1133 Palmerston to Russell. 19 May 1860. III, 230–231.

D/16 *Diary 1855*
23 January–7 February (extracts). III, 274–277.

---

[1] For access, see above, Appendix 3, p. 130.

[2] The property of the Broadlands Archives Trust. Temporarily deposited with the Historical Manuscripts Commission.

PEEL PAPERS.    The British Library.

BL ADD MS 40469    *Correspondence with WEG 1841–1842*
ff 156–157    WEG to Peel. 6 February 1842. I, 234–235.


RUSSELL PAPERS.    The Public Record Office.

PRO 30/22/14a    *Correspondence and papers of Lord John Russell 1 January–*
                 *2 November 1860*
167–170    WEG to Russell. 20 May 1860. III, 232–233.


PAPERS OF QUEEN VICTORIA.    The Royal Archives, Windsor
Castle.[1]

RA c48    *Papers relating to the ministerial crisis of 1873*
6    Memorandum by the Queen. 12 March 1873. IV, 28–
     29.
11    Memorandum by the Queen. 12 March 1873. IV, 29–
      30.
16    Memorandum by the Queen. 13 March 1873. IV, 31–
      32.
38    Memorandum by the Queen. 15 March 1873. IV, 34.


RA d26    *Papers relating to Ireland May–December 1869*
103    WEG to the Queen. 22 July 1869. IV, 15–16.


RA d27    *Papers relating to Ireland 1870–1872*
74    Memorandum by the Queen. 25 June 1871. IV, 20–21.


RA    *Journal 1868*
      5 December (extract). IV, 5–6.

---

[1] Access restricted.

# INDEX

Printed in Scotland by Her Majesty's Stationery Office at HMSO Press, Edinburgh
Dd 696322 C10 6/81 (17418)